Spanish

An Easy Way to Learn

Adalina Fuentes

NOTE: Some of you may experience difficulties with the pronunciation of the Spanish vowels, consonants, and syllables. To help you in this process, we suggest going to www.forvo.com.

This interactive site will assist you in learning to pronounce words correctly.

Table of Contents

Introduction

Welcome to the new, easy way of learning Spanish. If you are reading this book, it is likely that you have been looking for a lesson plan that not only teaches you the basics of the Spanish Language, but also guides you through the process of deeply understanding a complete new system of words and structures that are often tightly connected to the culture where they originate.

Learning a second language is important, but why Spanish? The motivations vary. Maybe you are driven by the economic opportunities that the Spanish market represents within your country. For example, in the US, the Hispanic population has reached well over 50 million* people and the projection for the year 2020 is an astonishing 60 million Hispanics or Latinos living in the country. They represent an important market in terms of economy and communication, and while most of these people will adopt the English Language, their heritage is a strong feature.

In terms of global communication, Spanish is the second most widely spoken language by number of native speakers, right after Chinese, coming second in a list of the most studied languages after English. It is quite likely that when you search for a piece of information online, you will come across articles, newspapers, and websites completely in Spanish, as the number of online sources in this language is increasing on a daily basis.

In terms of culture, the Spanish speaking world has so much to offer that it would be unfair to describe it in just a few words. From painters to writers, from food to history, the Spanish culture is so rich that it offers a palette of delight for anybody adventurous enough to embrace it.

It is clear that despite the difficulties associated with the structure and variations of the Spanish language, it is slowly becoming a powerful tool for communication, politics, the economy, and life in general.

The characteristics of the Spanish language, its pronunciation, and variations, make it a challenge for many people interested in learning it. However, we believe that with the right guidance and a positive attitude from the students, doubt vanishes and the challenge becomes a delightful experience that not only serves the purpose of learning a second language for practical reasons, but it opens the students' minds to a new, rich culture, encouraging contact with members of the Spanish-speaking world.

We can recognize the different types of Spanish across Latin America and this is a source of confusion for many speakers of other languages. It is commonly believed that the Spanish spoken in a certain region or country would be unintelligible for native Spanish speakers from a different country. However, the same can be said of the English language spoken in the UK, Australia, or the U.S. While it is true that each region or country has its own specific features, vocabulary, and phrases – for which localization is requested for many editorial and commercial products, it is possible to speak in a standard manner that will ensure communication is effective, fluent, and correct.

In this book, we focus on Standard Spanish that can be understood across all regions. This is the Spanish spoken at academic levels, as well as official communication, journalism, international business and media, and in everyday activities. We will also point out briefly the different meanings that a word can take, depending on the country where the word is spoken, with the intention to make the student aware of such variations and colloquialisms.

The overall purpose of this book series is to guide students in the process of learning Spanish, not just teach them a new language, but to use real life techniques and tips to improve the learning experience and make it permanent. We will include grammar notes and vocabulary in each lesson, as well as pronunciation patterns. We have carefully selected the best online resources where you can go to maximize your immersion in the language. A number of exercises complete this beginner's course for a fast, effective, easy, and fun learning process.

Dive in for the first easy Spanish lesson.

An Easy Start on Your Spanish

For those of you who would like to get started right away, either because you are leaving on a trip to Latin America or to Spain, or because you have met somebody who speaks perfect Spanish and would like to practice your skills with them, I will provide you with a number of useful phrases and words that you can easily learn so you won't be at a loss when trying to communicate in Spanish.

You will find these phrases and words grouped in categories so you can easily find them and get back to them whenever you need them! Let's get started!

Introducing Yourself

One of the first things that my students want to know in Spanish is how to introduce themselves to others. Maybe there is a common feeling all around the world that if you can say who you are in the language you are trying to learn, that is, a foreign language, then you show that you are indeed making an effort to facilitate communication, apart from it being a nice gesture.

This vocabulary will also help you get acquainted with the language and because the words and phrases are so short, they will provide a sense of comfort because you will convey a whole meaning with just a couple of words. I would like to add that native speakers love it when a foreigner introduces himself in Spanish so do not hesitate to use these phrases as soon as you get a chance!

Saying who you are

Sometimes you may be asked to say who you are. The following answers respond to the question:

¿Quién eres tú?, or / kien é-res tu/

¿Cuál es tu nombre?, or / kual es tu ´nom-bre/

¿Cómo te llamas? / ko-mo te ´lla-mas/

Soy Pedro / soi ´pe-dro *(I am Pedro)*

Mi nombre es Daniel / mi ´nom-bre es da-´niel *(My name is Daniel)*

Me llamo Lucía / me ´lla-mo lu-´ci-a *(My name is Lucia)*

Saying where you are from

If you want to state where you come from or if somebody asks you where you are from, you can use the following sentences:

¿De dónde eres? / de ´don-de ´e-res (*Where are you from?*)

Soy de Argentina / soi de ar-jen-´ti-na (*I'm from Argentina*)

Soy de Alemania / soi de a-le-´ma-nia (*I'm from Germany*)

Vengo de los Estados Unidos / ´ven-go de los es-´ta-dos u-´ni-dos (*I come from the US*)

General Greetings

Hola / o-la (*Hello – Hi*)

¿Cómo estás? / ´ko-mo es-´tas (*How are you? How are you doing?*)

¿Qué tal? / ke ´tal (*How is it going?*)

¿Cómo te va? / ´ko-mo te ´va (*How is it going?*)

¿Cómo está usted? / ´ko-mo es-´ta us-´ted (*How are you? (formal)*)

¿Cómo le va? / ´ko-mo le ´va (*How is it going? (formal)*)

Buenos días / ´bue-nos días (*Good morning*)

Buenas tardes / ´bue-nas ´tar-des (*Good afternoon*)

Buenas noches / ´bue-nas ´no ches (*Good evening*)

In many circumstances, you will find that a native speaker of Spanish uses a combination of two of these greetings. For some reason, it seems that one is not enough! So, an example of this would be:

Hola, ¿Qué tal? (*Hello, how are you?*)

Buenos días, ¿cómo está usted? (*Good morning, how are you doing?*)

Muy bien, gracias, ¿y usted? (*I'm fine, thanks, and you?*)

Some people will even greet you with three phrases. Here is an example:

Hola, ¿qué tal? Buen día.

This may sound odd, but it is quite common in informal situations.

Saying how old you are: In English, you need to use the verb "to be" in order to state your age: I'm 22.

But in Spanish, you will need to use a different verb to say how old you are: the irregular verb **Tener.**

Yo tengo 22 años

Because this is an irregular verb, I will give you the details about its conjugation so you know how to use it with the different subjects.

Verb: Tener (to have)

Yo tengo

Tú tienes

Él / Ella tiene

Nosotros tenemos

Ustedes tienen

Ellos tienen

If you add a number – plus the word **años** you can state your age or somebody else's.

So, if you want to greet somebody and give a little detail about yourself, you can say something like along these lines:

Hola, ¿Que tal? Mi nombre es Daniel. Tengo 30 años. Soy de Argentina.

Being Polite

These are some phases you can use to request something politely or to show gratitude.

Gracias / ´gra-cias (*Thank you*)

Muchas gracias / ´mu-chas ´gra-cias (*Thank you very much*)

De nada - por nada - no hay de qué /de ´na-da/ /por ´na-da/ / no ai de ke (*You're welcome*)

Por favor / por fa-´vor (*Please*)

Lo siento / lo ´sien-to (*I'm sorry*)

Disculpe / dis-´kul-pe (*Pardon me*)

Numbers – Part I

Because numbers are part of our everyday life, I thought you might find it useful to know just a little bit about them in this introductory section. You will definitely benefit from reading and learning the more comprehensive list of numbers and how they are written at the end of this book in the vocabulary section, but for now, here are numbers 0 – 10 and how to pronounce them.

0 – cero / ´ce-ro/

1- uno / ´u-no/

2 – dos / dos/

3 – tres / tres/

4 – cuatro / ´kua-tro/

5 – cinco / ´cin-ko/

6 – seis / seis/

7 –siete / ´sie-te/

8 – ocho / ´o-cho/

9 – nueve / ´nue-ve/

10 – diez / diez/

At The Airport

The following words and phrases will come in handy when you have just arrived to your destination.

¿Dónde está mi equipaje? / ´don-de es-´ta mi e-ki-´pa-je (*Where is my luggage?*)

¿Dónde está la aduana? / ´don-de es-´ta la a-´dua-na (*Where is customs?*)

¿Dónde está la mesa de información? / ´don-de es-´ta la ´me-sa de in-for-ma-´cion (*Where is the information desk?*)

¿Dónde reclamo mi equipaje? / ´don-de re-´kla-mo mi e-ki-´pa-je (*Where do I claim my luggage?*)

¿Dónde puedo comprar un boleto? / ´don-de ´pue-do kom-´prar un bo-´le-to (*Where can I buy a ticket?*)

¿Hay taxis hacia la ciudad? / ai ´tac-sis ´a-cia la ´ciu-dad (*Is there a taxi to go to the city?*)

¿Hay un autobús hacia la ciudad? / ai un au-to-´bus ´a-cia la ´ciu-dad (*Is there a bus service to the city?*)

¿Dónde está la oficina de turismo? / ´don-de es-´ta la o-fi-´ci-na de tu´ris-mo (*Where is the tourist office?*)

At The Hotel

How do you book a room? How do you ask for the bill? How do you ask for particular amenities? This list of useful words and phrases will help you!

Tengo una reserva / ´ten-go ´u-na re-´ser-va (*I have a reservation*)

Quiero una habitación, por favor / ´kie-ro ´u-na a-bi-ta-´cion por fa-´vor (*I would like a room, please*)

Una habitación para una persona / ´u-na a-bi-ta-´cion ´pa-ra ´u-na per-´so-na (*A room for one*)

Una habitación para dos personas / ´u-na a-bi-ta-´cion ´pa-ra dos per-´so-nas (*A room for two*)

Estaré una noche / es-ta-´re ´u-na ´no-che (*I will stay for one night*)

Estaré tres noches / es-ta-´re tres ´no-ches (*I will stay for three nights*)

Estaré una semana / es-ta-´re ´u-na se-´ma-na (*I will stay for a week*)

Una habitación con aire acondicionado / ´u-na a-bi-ta-´cion kon ´ai-re a-kon-di-cio-´na-do (*A room with air-conditioning*)

Una habitación con vista / ´u-na a-bi-ta-´cion kon ´vis-ta (*A room with a view*)

Una habitación estándard / ´u-na a-bi-ta-´cion es-´tan-dar (*A standard room*)

Una habitación superior / ´u-na a-bi-ta-´cion su-pe-´rior (*An upgraded room*)

La cuenta por favor / la ´kuen-ta por fa-´vor (*Can I have the bill, please?*)

At The Restaurant

Quiero ir a un buen restaurante / ´kie-ro ir a un buen res-tau-´ran-te (*I want to go to a good restaurant*)

¿Cuál es un buen restaurante? / kual es un buen res-tau-´ran-te (*Which one is a good restaurant?*)

El menú, por favor / el me-´nu por fa-´vor (*The menu, please*)

¿Donde está el baño? / ´don-de es-´ta el ´ba-nio (*Where is the restroom?*)

Me gustaría ordenar / me gus-ta-´ria or-de-´nar (*I would like to have/order*)

Entrada – aperitivo / en-´tra-da/ /a-pe-ri-´ti-vo (*Appetizers*)

Plato principal / ´pla-to prin-ci-´pal (*Main course*)

Postre / ´pos-tre (*Dessert*)

Pollo / ´po-llo (*Chicken*)

Mariscos / ma-´ris-kos (*Seafood*)

Comida vegetariana / ko-´mi-da ve-je-ta-´ria-na (*Vegetarian food*)

Carne / ´kar-ne (*Steak*)

Cerdo / ´cer-do (*Pork*)

Pasta / ´pas-ta (*Pasta*)

Ensaladas / en-sa-´la-das (*Salads*)

Vino / ´vi-no (*Wine*)

Cerveza / cer-´ve-za (*Beer*)

Gaseosa / ga-´seo-sa (*Soft drink / soda*)

Café / ka-´fe (*Coffee*)

La cuenta, por favor / la ´kuen-ta por fa-´vor (*Check, please*)

Transportation

The following vocabulary is useful for getting around the city. Know the words and you will be able to travel or even ask for directions!

Taxi / ´tak-si (*Cab; taxi*)

Autobus / au-to-´bus (*Bus*)

Parada del autobus / pa-´ra-da del au-to-´bus (*Bus stop*)

Tren / tren (*Train*)

Estación de trenes / es-ta-´cion de ´tre-nes (*Train station*)

Avión / a-´vion (*Plane*)

Automóvil / au-to-´mo-vil (*Car*)

Barco / ´bar-ko (*Ship*)

Some useful phrases

Tomar el autobús / to-´mar el au-to-´bus (*To take the bus*)

Tomar el tren / to-´mar el ´tren (*To take the train*)

Subir abordo de un barco / su-´bir a-´bor-do de un ´bar-ko (*To board a ship*)

Abordar el avión / a-bor-´dar el a-´vion (*To board the plane*)

Tomar un taxi / to-´mar un ´tac-si (*To take a cab*)

Asking for directions

When you are in a Spanish speaking country, you can ask for directions with the following phrases:

¿En qué dirección está el museo? / en ke di-rec-'sion es-'ta el mu-'se-o (*Which way is the museum?*)

¿Dónde está el banco? / 'don-de es-'ta el 'ban-ko (*Where is the bank?*)

¿Dónde está el parque? / 'don-de es-'ta el 'par-ke (*Where is the park?*)

¿En qué dirección está la iglésia? / en ke di-rec-'sion es-'ta la i-'gle-sia (*Which way is the church?*)

Está a dos cuadras / es-'ta a dos 'kua-dras (*It's two blocks away*)

Está a la derecha / es-'ta a la de-'re-cha (*It's on the right*)

Está a la izquierda / es-'ta a la iz-'kier-da (*It's on the left*)

Está siguiendo esta calle / es-'ta si-'guien-do 'es-ta 'ka-lle (*It's straight ahead*)

At The Store

¿Cuanto cuesta esto? / ´kuan-to ´kues-ta ´es-to (*How much is this?*)

¿Cual es el precio de esto? / kual es el ´pre-cio de ´es-to (*What is its price?*)

Quiero uno / ´kie-ro ´u-no (*I will have one*)

Quiero dos / ´kie-ro dos (*I will have two*)

¿Tiene otros colores? / ´tie-ne ´o-tros ko-´lo-res (*Do you have this in other colors?*)

¿Tiene otros tamaños? / ´tie-ne ´o-tros ta-´ma-nio (*Do you have this in a different size?*)

Lo llevaré / lo lle-va-´re (*I will take it*)

Health and Safety

What to say in case there is an emergency:

!Ayuda! / a-ýu-da (*Help*)

¡Un doctor, por favor! / un dok-ʹtor por fa-ʹvor (*I need a doctor, please!*)

¡Llame a una ambulancia! / ʹlla-me a ʹu-na am-bu-ʹlan-cia (*Call an ambulance!*)

¡Llame a los bomberos! / ʹlla-me a los bom-ʹbe-ros (*Call the fire department!*)

Estoy enfermo / es-ʹtoi en-ʹfer-mo (*I'm sick*)

Infarto / in-ʹfar-to (*Heart attack*)

Dolor de Cabeza – Jaqueca / do-ʹlor de ka-ʹbe-za/ /ja-ke-ka (*Headache*)

Dolor de estómago / do-ʹlor de es-ʹto-ma-go (*Stomachache*)

Me robaron / me ro-ʹba-ron (*I've been robbed*)

Estoy lastimado / es-ʹtoi las-ti-ʹma-do (*I am hurt*)

Estoy perdido / es-ʹtoi per-ʹdi-do (*I am lost*)

Grammar Unit 1: Subject Pronouns

How do we learn a language? When students come to the classroom, they seem to forget that they have already gone through the learning process once: when they were kids. Our mother tongue comes to us in a natural learning environment. We take it in by repetition, by making mistakes, being corrected, and by listening to other people speak. We do not realize that our mother tongue is a complex system of structures, ideas, words, and functions until we go to school and start analyzing sentences. When learning a language, it is important to acquire the structures and then to forget about them. How is this possible? Why should you forget about grammar structures? Because the goal is to be so familiarized with them that they become internal and you do not have to think about them when you speak, just like you do when you utter a sentence in your native language.

In order to start creating sentences - and speaking in Spanish - I invite you to take a look at some of the elements that form a sentence. Read the following example:

She is young.

In the above sentence, you can identify a subject (she), a conjugated verb (is), and an adjective (young). This sentence presents a basic structure. Now take a look at the sentence in Spanish:

Ella es joven.

In the above sentence again, you can find a subject (ella), a conjugated verb (es), and an adjective (joven). Easy - right? Basic sentences in Spanish will take a simple structure formed by a subject and a predicate - what is said about that subject - for example, the action he or she performs.

Personal pronouns replace the subject of the sentence. They take the place of the main subject or subjects. For example, instead of saying **María**, you can use **she**.

Read the following list of personal pronouns in Spanish and their equivalents in English.

Yo *(I)*

Tú / Usted *(You)*

Él (He) / Ella *(She)*

Nosotros *(We)*

Vosotros / Ustedes *(You)*

Ellos *(They)*

As you can see, the first three pronouns are singular and the last three are plural. There is no specific pronoun that can be considered equivalent to **it** and for this reason, certain sentences will be called **impersonal** where the subject is simply omitted. We will tackle these later in this book. Take a look at the following examples:

Él sabe cantar *(He can sing)*

Nosotros estamos bien *(We are alright)*

Ella es alemana *(She is German)*

Yo sé nadar *(I can swim)*

Tú eres muy listo *(You are clever)*

Ellos hablan rápido *(They speak fast)*

Ustedes están felices *(You are happy)*

In the above sentences, the English and Spanish structures are very similar and although this may be found in some simple affirmative sentences, it is not the general rule for complex predications. However, basic structure formation for Spanish sentences is:

Subject – Verb – Object

Example:

Ella come chocolate. *(She eats chocolate)*

In every stage of learning a new language, I always recommend my students to practice, practice, and practice as much as possible. For every lesson, I will give you tips about how to best incorporate the new knowledge so you find it easy and can start seeing results right away.

For this lesson, I recommend that you say out loud or whisper in your head the personal pronoun for everybody you see. For example, if you are at the theater and a group of people come in, you can say or think of: Ellos (they); if you are at the cafeteria and a girl comes in, make it a custom to say: E lla (she); if you go to the bar and you are waiting for a guy friend, when he arrives you can say: Él. These simple steps will help you get started on the new language and will **anchor** the new structures and knowledge.

Remember - when possible, do not try to think of the English word first. I do not want you to constantly translate English into Spanish in your mind; I want you to really start thinking in Spanish.

Notes about the Spanish personal pronouns

In Spanish, there are two different ways of referring to the second person singular, **you**, depending on the relationship between you, the speaker, and the recipient of the message:

Tú *(you)*

Usted *(you)*

We use **Tú** when we are familiar with the person we are speaking to or if they are a friend, a relative, or a workmate. It denotes closeness and it's an informal way of addressing somebody.

We use **Usted** when we want to show respect towards somebody and it is a formal way of addressing somebody. This is used for speaking to older people, somebody in authority, or with a higher rank (for example, a boss, although this is slowly changing for a more informal **tú**).

Look at these examples:

Tu eres mi amigo – informal – *(You are my friend)*

Usted puede entrar – formal – *(You can come in)*

Gender in some personal pronouns

Take a look at these pronouns:

Ellos/Ellas (*They*)

Nosotros/Nosotras (*We*)

Vosotros/Vosotras or Ustedes (*You*)

In Spanish, the issue of gender is present in adjectives, determiners, demonstratives, and pronouns. In general, I teach my students that the final vowel **–a** indicates female gender, and **-o** or **-e** usually indicate male gender, although you will see that sometimes this rule is broken. In the case of pronouns, there are two variations depending on the gender we refer to.

If you want to talk about two or more people where you are not included, you can use ellos if the group is comprised of men only and ellas if the group is made up of women only. However, if the group is mixed – men and women- you will use the general word ellos.

The same happens with the pronoun we. If you are talking about a group of two or more people where you are included, you will use the word nosotros if the group is made up of men only or men and women. But if the two people or more are women, you will use nosotras.

Exercises

Now, let's work on some simple exercises to help you get started on the personal pronouns. Do not worry about the part of the sentence that you don't know (the predicate), we will get to that as we progress on this course for beginners.

Exercise 1: Use the correct personal pronoun.

a. Carmen, Lucía y Sabrina: _____

b. Yo (male), Lucía y Sabrina: _____

c. José: _____

d. Monica y José: _____

e. Mónica y María: _____

f. Yo (female), Fiona y Lucas: _____

g. Lucas y José: _____

h. Yo (female), Fiona y Mónica: _____

Exercise 2: The following sentences show names of people and what they do. Replace the name(s) with the correct personal pronoun:

a. Laura enseña arte en la universidad. *Laura teaches art at University.*

a. _____ enseña arte en la universidad.

b. Roberto conduce su auto. *Roberto drives his car.*

b. _____ conduce su auto.

c. María y José viajan en avión. *María and Jose travel by plain.*

c. _____ viajan en avión.

d. Pedro no toma café. *Pedro doesn't drink coffe*

d. _____ no toma café.

e. Yo, Lucas y Lory miramos TV. *Lucas, Lory and I watch TV.*

e. _____ miramos TV.

f. Silvia canta por la mañana. *Silvia sings in the morning.*

f. _____ canta por la mañana.

g. Lucy compra algunas manzanas. *Lucy is buying some apples.*

g. _____ compra algunas manzanas.

h. Tomás prepara la cena. *Tomas prepares dinner.*

h. _____ prepara la cena.

i. Mauricio lee el diario. *Mauricio reads the newspaper.*

i. _____ lee el diario.

j. Lorena, María y Lucy llegan mañana. *Lorena, Maria and Lucy arrive tomorrow.*

j. _____ llegan mañana.

At the end of the book, you will find the <u>Unit 1</u> Key with the correct answers so you can check your progress.

Grammar Unit 2: Gender of Nouns

One lesson that my students often find intriguing is the issue of Noun Gender. In Spanish, as opposed to English, nouns are either male or female, whether they are abstract (like hope, happiness, idealism, etc.) or concrete (such as dog, door, building, etc.). In the following pages, I will teach you how to recognize a male or female noun in Spanish and you will find a list of exceptions to memorize.

Let's start from the beginning. Think of some nouns in English. In case you do not remember what a noun is, it names people, places, things, and ideas. You may include in your list: marathon, cup, tie, journal, dress, remote control, and stairs. Could you describe these nouns in terms of gender? Probably not, especially if English is your mother tongue. Normally, English speakers cannot distinguish gender in nouns and this is okay because it is not a part of their culture.

When I introduced this course book, I mentioned that any language is often tightly related to the culture that embraces it and Spanish is not the exception. Noun gender is a very important feature of the Spanish language and something that you will master with time and practice.

Take a look at the following nouns:

Mes**a** *(Table)*

Cas**a** *(House)*

Vel**a** *(Candle)*

Alegrí**a** *(Joy)*

Would you say these are feminine or masculine? There is no reasoning that we can apply to the gender usage of a noun, but we can look at some of the patterns that form a feminine or masculine noun.

In class, I ask my students to pay attention at words, especially when they are unfamiliar with them. Do not look at them as just "items" in a text - analyze them, divide them, and try to find the patterns, the logic behind some of them, and their roots. This is a useful and fun resource for making progress, while learning.

In the previous list, I have highlighted the last letter of each word. The **–a** ending designates - **in most cases** - a feminine noun. I will teach you some exceptions and you may find some of your own as you go through material outside of this book, such as newspapers, magazines or websites; but for now, this is a rule you need to pay attention to.

Now you will find a different list:

Barco *(Ship)*

Chaleco *(Vest)*

Asiento *(Seat)*

Diente *(Tooth)*

Again, take a look at the bold ending of each word. Nouns that end in **–o** or **–e** are - **in most cases** - masculine. There are exceptions to this rule and I will provide a list as we progress in this lesson.

These are two simple rules that you can use to identify the gender of a noun. My students often wonder, what is the point in knowing the noun gender? To form sentences, to name things, and to express what is in your mind, you need to know vocabulary, as well as grammar. The English language, as well as other languages around the world, does not distinguish gender in nouns, but if you wish to write or speak Spanish, you need to know the rules in order to express your ideas clearly.

In addition to the endings of a noun word (-**o** and –**e** for masculine, -**a** for feminine), you will often find a definite article in front of the noun. An article is a part of speech used to indicate something - that something is a noun. In English, we use **the** as a definite article, whereas in Spanish, we use two forms (four if we include the plurals – we will take a look at these later): **el** and **la**.

The definite articles el and la precede the noun, they *define* it.

El is used for masculine nouns and **la** is used for feminine nouns. I will use the list above and include the definite article so you can compare:

El barc**o** *(The ship)*

El chaleco *(The vest)*

El asiento *(The seat)*

El diente *(The tooth)*

La mesa *(The table)*

La casa *(The house)*

La vela *(The candle)*

La alegría *(The joy)*

As you can see, the gender of a noun is not in fact within the noun, it is not a characteristic that you can determine by its shape, use, or origin. I recommend that you think first of the ending of a word, before deciding which definite article is appropriate for that word in particular. On the other side, if you hear or read the definite article first, you can predict the gender of the noun and often its ending.

My students of Spanish often find it useful to relate these new rules to something they already know. For examples, I mentioned that nouns include people, things, places, and ideas. I recommend using examples with people, pets, or animals in order to clarify any doubt and fix the new knowledge to your *personal library*.

Masculine / Feminine

Tío *(Uncle)* / Tía *(Aunt)*

Niño *(Boy)* / Niña *(Girl)*

Conejo *(Rabbit)* / Coneja *(Rabbit)*

Abogado *(Lawyer)* / Abogada *(Lawyer)*

You can add the definite article **el/la** before each noun and check that it coincides:

Masculine / Feminine

El tí**o** *(The uncle)* / La tí**a** *(Aunt)*

El niñ**o** *(The boy)* / La niñ**a** *(Girl)*

El conej**o** *(The rabbit)* / La conej**a** *(The rabbit)*

El abogad**o** *(Lawyer)* / La abogad**a** *(Lawyer)*

Once you feel comfortable with these terms, you can move on the next part of this lesson and that is, nouns with different endings and their gender.

I recently taught you that nouns ending in –a are feminine in Spanish. **Other endings** that convey feminine gender for nouns are:

-tud, -tad, -dad:

L**a** esclavit**ud** *(The slavery)*

L**a** liber**tad** *(The freedom)*

L**a** simplici**dad** *(The simplicity)*

In other words, these nouns will take **la** as a definite article. Read the list and write notes about it. Try to memorize it, take your time, but do make an effort. It will pay off at the end of the lesson.

-ción, -sión, -gión (and most words ending in –ión):

L**a** revolu**ción** *(The revolution)*

L**a** profe**sión** *(The profession)*

L**a** le**gión** *(The legion)*

-triz

L**a** empera**triz** *(The empress)*

La ac**triz** *(The actress)*

La institu**triz** *(The governess)*

-ez (for abstract nouns):

La delgad**ez** *(The slimness)*

La estupid**ez** *(The stupidity)*

La sencill**ez** *(The simplicity/modesty)*

-umbre:

La servid**umbre** *(The servitude)*

La cost**umbr**e *(The custom)*

La podred**umbre** *(The rottenness)*

In the previous pages, I said that nouns ending in **–e** and **–o** are masculine and take **el** as a definite article. However, there is one particular rule that you must know and a few examples.

-ma (most of these nouns are of Greek origins)

El cli**ma** *(The weather)*

El te**ma** *(The topic)*

El dra**ma** *(The drama)*

Also other nouns ending in **–a** are masculine:

El día *(The day)*

El sof**á** *(The sofa)*

El map**a** *(The map)*

El planet**a** *(The planet)*

These are exceptions and you should memorize them as there are only four. You can also use them to recall the opposite rule: nouns ending in **–a** are feminine.

I will show you now two categories that may be considered *easier* to learn:

The following words do not have a specific gender and it can only be determined by the definite article that precedes it:

El/la cli**ente** *(The client)*

El/la estudi**ante** *(The student)*

El/la paci**ente** *(The patient)*

El/la art**ista** *(The artist)*

El/la pas**ante** *(The intern)*

El/la buró**crata** *(The burocrat)*

As a general rule, you will find that nouns ending in **–ista, -ante, -ente, -crata** are used either for masculine or feminine nouns and the gender depends on the preceding definite article, **el** or **la**.

Another category that my students like because of its simplicity is comprised of nouns that end in a consonant. Regularly, these nouns are masculine when they end in a consonant and to turn it into feminine you must add **–a**. Look at the following examples:

El orador / La orado**ra** *(The public speaker)*

El directo**r** / La directo**ra** *(The director)*

El ladró**n** / La ladro**na** *(The thief)*

El presentado**r** / La presentado**ra** *(The host)*

Theory can sometimes be overwhelming and my goal is to help you find ways to make it easier. Some lessons will have points of comparison with the English language or structures that you can easily identify and use. Other parts of the program will require an active learner. My suggestion for this lesson is that you keep a notebook next to you when you read it and write down the rules and a few examples for each of them. Writing will help you memorize them and it should only take you 1-2 minutes. Short lists of nouns will help you see the rules in action and at the same time, it will only take you a moment to go over them again when you need to. Additionally, I ask my students to search for newspaper or magazine articles, cut them and paste them on the same page as the rules on your notebook and highlight or circle the endings we just learned. It does not matter at this point if you understand the rest of the article, just focus on the nouns. When you see a word with the above endings or a definite article el/la, look it up in a dictionary to check that it is indeed a noun and circle it. This simple exercise will help you become familiarized with the words and texts in Spanish. Before you know it, you will become comfortable with finding and reading Spanish words in a text.

Exercises

Now it's time you check your recently gained knowledge. Don't worry if you can't get it right from the start. Write the answers with a pencil and erase them when you are wrong. Give yourself some time to review the rules and after 1-2 days, try to complete them again. This way you will fix the knowledge in your mind effectively.

Exercise 1: Male or female? Some can be both.

a. bota (boot) _____

b. mensaje (message) _____

c. maestro (teacher) _____

d. cliente (client) _____

e. gato (cat) _____

f. fiesta (party) _____

g. automóvil (car) _____

h. estudiante (student) _____

i. asistente (assistant) _____

j. ropa (clothes) _____

k. costumbre (custom) _____

l. decisión (decision) _____

m. felicidad (happiness) _____

n. tema (topic) _____

Exercise 2: Add the definite article to each noun:

a. _____ drama (drama)

b. _____ asesor (consultant)

c. _____ mueble (furniture)

d. _____ amistad (friendship)

e. _____ ciudad (city)

f. _____ carta (letter)

g. _____ legumbre (legume)

h. _____ religión (religion)

i. _____ canción (song)

j. _____ intendente (mayor)

At the end of the book, you will find the Unit 2 Key with the correct answers so you can check your progress.

Spanish Words You Didn't Know You Knew...

Some words are quite similar both in English and Spanish, which makes them learn! Here are some examples to start with:

Abandon- abandonar   Academic- académico

Adapt- adaptar   Adult- adulto

Grammar Unit 3: Plural nouns

This is a very popular lesson in the classroom because it is easy to remember and you can start practicing right away. I am going to teach you how to form the plural of nouns. Some of the nouns belong to the previous lesson and you are already familiarized with them.

Let's start with a simple rule. For nouns that end in a vowel, you simply add –s at the end:

Elefant**e** /Elefant**es** *(Elephant)*

Mes**a** / Mes**as** *(Table)*

Barc**o** / Barc**os** *(Ship)*

As you can see, once you identify the nouns, you will determine how to form the plural by looking at their endings.

When the nouns end in a consonant, you will need to add –**es**. Take a look at the examples:

Profeso**r** / Profesor**es** *(Professor)*

Televiso**r** / Televisor**es** *(Television)*

Silló**n** / sillon**es** *(Couch)*

In Spanish, most common nouns will end in –**r**, -**n**, -**d**, -**s**. You may however come across other examples with different consonant endings.

Another category I teach my students is nouns ending with –**z**. In this case, you will need to replace the –z with a –**c**, and then add –**es**. It is not as complicated as it may sound! Take a look:

Actri**z** / Actri**ces** *(Actress)*

Avestru**z** / Avestru**ces** *(Ostrich)*

Lu**z** / Lu**ces** *(Light)*

For nouns ending in **–ión**, you will have to add **–es**. Most verbs with this ending will take an accent (such as canción, promoción) so make sure you drop it before adding **–es** to make it orthographically correct.

Here are some examples:

Revolu**ión** / Revolu**ciones** (Revolution)

Profes**ión** / Profes**iones** (Profession)

Cam**ión** / Cam**iones** (Truck)

Some nouns are always plural in Spanish and you should use them with the correct definite article. I recommend my students to make a list of these nouns so you can remember them easier and you can add more as you come across them while making progress in your studies.

Always Plural nouns:

Las tijeras *(The scissors)*

Los pantalones *(The trousers)*

Los anteojos *(The glasses)*

Notice that we used a new form of the definite article. These are the plural definite articles and I will teach you more about them in the next lesson.

The world of nouns is interesting and a great way to get your feet wet in the Spanish language. By now, you must have noticed that there is a lot to learn and rules cannot always be compared to those in the English language. Therefore, you need to think of them as a whole new system and aim at knowing them without a constant comparison or reference to your mother tongue.

Exercises

Please complete the following exercises based on the lesson you just learned.

Exercise 1 Plural or Singular?

a. libros _____

b. soga _____

c. autos _____

d. televisores _____

e. mesas _____

f. libertad _____

g. avión _____

h. pantalones _____

i. lápiz _____

j. canción _____

Exercise 2: Make the following nouns plural.

a. vaso _____

b. letra _____

c. persona _____

d. bolso _____

e. juego _____

f. profesora _____

g. pasión _____

h. camino _____

i. viaje _____

j. matiz _____

k. chocolate _____

l. mansión _____

m. sabor _____

n. dulce _____

o. sillón _____

p. actriz _____

q. mapa _____

r. amigo _____

s. ratón _____

t. uva _____

u. salón _____

v. barco _____

w. manzana _____

x. avión _____

At the end of the book, you will find the <u>Unit 3</u> Key with the correct answers so you can check your progress.

How To Say...?

When you need help...   ¿Puede ayudarme? /puede ayuˈdarme/

Grammar Unit 4: Definite and Indefinite Articles

One of the first things you need to know in Spanish is how to name things and while this is part of the lesson on nouns, you quickly learned that you do not only need to call things by their name, but you also need to use something in front of the noun to define it. That something is called the definite and indefinite articles and I am going to teach you all about them in this lesson.

In English, the definite article is the word **the**. It is called so because it **defines** the noun that it precedes. You already know this instinctively or from school so it will not be difficult to revisit it now that you are learning Spanish. We use **the** in front of a noun to name a particular item and **define** it. For example, if you say **I saw the kid by the church**, you are talking about a particular kid, maybe a boy or girl that you were discussing before, or even a child that somebody else mentioned before. You did not see **any** kid by the church, you saw **that kid** that everybody knows about from the context where the sentence is said. The meaning is different when you say **I saw a kid by the church**. In this case, it means that a child, any child, was near the church and you are not specifying who he or she was. If you were not aware of this difference before, you will be now as we learn to name things in Spanish.

Because the Spanish language distinguishes male and female gender in nouns, we will have to use a more complex set of definite and indefinite articles, but do not worry! You will see that they are quite easy to remember and as long as you do the practice exercises, you will learn them really fast!

Definite article in English: The

This single word defines a noun. It is a definite article.

Definite articles in Spanish: **el, la, los, las**.

In Spanish, we use four different forms of the definite article depending on the gender and number of the noun it precedes. Look at the following examples:

El niño *(The boy)*

La niña *(The girl)*

Los niños *(The boys)*

Las niñas *(The girls)*

In the examples above, you can notice that **el** and **la** are used for singular nouns, male and female respectively. Then, **los** and **las** are used for plural nouns, male and female respectively.

Let's see more examples.

El profesor *(The teacher (male))*

La profesora *(The teacher (female))*

Los profesores *(The teachers (male))*

Las profesoras *(The teachers (female))*

Slowly you will learn to think in advance the type of noun you will use in order to choose the correct article, definite or indefinite, according to gender and number. My students often find it difficult to distinguish male from female articles and that is a common mistake among Spanish as a Second Language students. But it is also one that you can easily overcome by paying attention and learning to recognize the nouns.

Definite article singular:

El doctor / **La** doctora *(The doctor)*

Definite article plural:

Los doctores / **Las** doctoras *(The doctors)*

One thing to take into account is which definite article to use when you need to name a group of elements. In Spanish, when there is a mixed group of elements, male and female, the masculine articles are used. For examples, if there is a mixed group of doctors performing a surgery, the masculine article is used:

Los doctores operaron a Susana *(The doctors performed surgery on Susana)*

(There were 2 male doctors and 2 female doctors).

The number of each gender participants in a group is irrelevant, as long as there is one male component, the masculine article is used.

Indefinite article

In English, we will use the indefinite articles **a**, **an** and **some** to refer to any object without singling it out. Look at the following examples to see the difference:

I sat on a chair – indefinite

*I sat on the (old / elegant / broken / green / et.) chair – **definite***

The indefinite article is used to refer to any object without any particular reference to it.

In Spanish, we have a number of words that can be used in this way, again - depending on the gender and number of the noun they precede. One of my students said once that this is a cool feature of the Spanish language because it adds variety and gives you a completely different approach to everyday objects.

So, with this positive attitude, let's take a look at the indefinite articles in Spanish:

Un – *(a/an)* indefinite, male singular

Una – *(a/an)* indefinite, female singular

Unos – *(some)* indefinite, male plural

Unas – *(some)* indefinite, female plural

These examples will give you a better perspective on how to use them:

Un libro (*a book)* / Unos libros (*Some books)*

Una planta (*a plant)* / Unas plantas (*Some plants)*

As you can see, **un** and **una** are equivalent to **a** and **an**, only that the change depends on the noun gender, as opposed to the first letter of the noun they precede. When the noun calls for an indefinite plural article, the words **unos** and **unas** are used, in comparison with **some** in English.

Remember that the purpose of comparing the structures to the English language is so that you can incorporate them more easily and have some kind of reference, but the main goal is to learn to think in Spanish and not translate from English into Spanish every time you want to speak.

Although it may seem childish, some images or drawings may help you remember these variations. In your notes, draw or paste a picture of different object and write down whether they are singular or plural.

For example, take a picture of your dog/dogs and write down: el perro / los perros / la perra / las perras, depending on their gender and number. Do not write it in English, use only Spanish.

Exercises

Exercise 1: Complete with the right definite article.

a. ____ teléfono *(telephone)*

b. ____ sillones *(sofas)*

c. ____ niña *(girl)*

d. ____mujeres *(women)*

e. ____libros *(books)*

f. ____libreta *(notebook)*

g.____ lápiz *(pencil)*

h. ____fiesta *(party)*

i. ____leones *(lions)*

j. ____corazón *(heart)*

k. ____profesoras *(teachers)*

l. ____doctores *(doctors)*

m. ____diccionario *(dictionary)*

n. ____platos *(plates)*

Exercise 2: Definite or Indefinite?

a. la _____

b. una _____

c. los _____

d. unas _____

e. el _____

f. un _____

g. los _____

h. unos _____

Exercise 3: The following articles do not match the noun. Write them in the correct form, using the right article.

a. Los libro _____

b. La profesor _____

c. Un gatos _____

d. Una flores _____

e. El bandera _____

f. Los casa _____

g. Una televisor _____

h. El cama _____

i. Un galletitas _____

At the end of the book, you will find the Unit 4 Key with the correct answers so you can check your progress.

Spanish Words You Didn't Know You Knew...

Alarm- alarma

Atack- atacar

Barbecue-barbacoa

Animal- animal

Baby- bebé

Brilliant- brillante

Grammar Unit 5: Verb Haber in Spanish

In Spanish, we use the verb **haber** to express availability. You can use it to talk about people, things, and even abstract nouns like the ones we studied before. Haber in Spanish is equivalent to **there is** and **there are** in English and you will notice that there is only one conjugation in the present, the form **hay**, as opposed to English. So, to put it in other words, you do not need to think of the noun in terms of plural or singular in order to use the verb **haber** because the form **hay** will be used for both in the present. Take a look at these examples:

Hay una niña en el scenario *(There is a girl on the stage)*

Hay tres perros en la plaza *(There are three dogs at the park)*

As you can see, the same conjugated form is used in both cases. At class, my students love this lesson because this is the first verb that you will be learning and it is fairly easy to use. I believe this is a great introduction to the Spanish language and at the same time, you can start using it right away, naming things in the room where you are studying right now. Once you read this lesson thoroughly, go to the vocabulary units and start practicing by saying what there is around you!

The verb **haber** and its conjugated form **hay**, can be used in multiple tenses and in affirmative, negative, and interrogative forms, just like any other verb. Take a look at these examples:

Hay 20 habitaciones en este hotel. *(There are 20 rooms in this hotel)*

¿Hay 6 personas en la casa? *(Are there 6 people in the house?)*

No hay leche en la heladera *(There isn't any milk in the fridge)*

To form the interrogative questions, you must place the conjugated verb **hay** at the beginning of the sentence or before the noun and immediately afterwards, the phrase that indicates location.

In the above sentences, **en este hotel** (in this hotel), **en la casa** (in the house), and **en la heladera** (in the fridge), indicate location. This part of the sentence will usually come after the noun.

Now, take a look around you. What can you see? Are there any plants, a TV, a telephone? Can you see a couch, people, pets? Try saying the following sentences:

Hay una planta sobre la mesa *(There is a plant on the table)*

Hay dos perros cerca de la puerta *(There are two dogs by the door)*

Hay un sillón en la sala *(There is a couch in the living room)*

Hay dos niños en el jardín *(There are two kids in the garden)*

Hay queso en la heladera *(There is cheese in the fridge)*

The verb **haber** is also used in impersonal sentences to express that something is needed or that something must be done. The following examples show you how to use the verb in this way:

Hay que regar las plantas *(It is necessary to water the plants)*

Hay que trabajar *(It is necessary to work)*

Hay que llevar a los niños al colegio *(It is necessary to take the kids to school)*

As you can see in the examples above, the conjugated form **hay** is followed by the relative pronoun **que** and an infinitive form of the verb (to work, to take, to water). If you feel this is confusing, remember that grammar structures in Spanish are quite different from English and you need to learn them as native speakers do: by repetition, trial, and error.

At this stage, you may not know every word in this lesson, but you will greatly benefit from reading the vocabulary section at the end of this book. Make sure you refer to it every time a new word comes up. Making flashcards is also helpful. You can cut out some pieces of paper in squares and write down notes to help you become familiar with the new knowledge.

Write short sentences and read them often, while you have breakfast, while commuting, before going to sleep or when you are bored! I will share more games that you can use to learn Spanish in the easiest possible way.

Exercises

Now, let's practise!

Exercise 1: Take a look around you. Say whether the following items are in the room. Write affirmative and negative sentences.

a. Una TV (a TV) _____

b. Perfume (a perfume) _____

c. Gato (a cat) _____

d. Planta (a plant) _____

e. Heladera (a refrigerator) _____

f. Sillón (a couch) _____

g. Plato (a plate) _____

h. Teléfono (a telephone) _____

i. Estantería (a shelf) _____

j. Sillas (chairs) _____

Exercise 2: The speaker describes what he is seeing. Use the verb "haber" plus the cues to form sentences. You may need to review the lesson on numbers in order to write them in Spanish. First read the example and then complete the exercise:

a. Example: I can see two cats on the roof - Hay dos gatos en el techo

b. I can see a kid in the garden - _____ niño en el jardín

c. I can see two people in the street - _____ personas en la calle

d. I can see five chairs in the room - _____ sillas en la sala

e. I can see three schools in the neighborhood - _____ escuelas en el barrio

f. I can see a book on the table - _____ libro sobre la mesa

g. I can see a computer on the desk - _____ computadora en el escritorio

h. I can see two TVs in the house - _____ TVs en la casa

i. I can see a comb in my purse - _____ peine en mi cartera

j. I can see a painting on the wall - _____ cuadro en la pared

At the end of the book, you will find the Unit 5 Key with the correct answers so you can check your progress.

Spanish Words You Didn't Know You Knew

Cable cable	Calculate calcular
Calendar calendario	Celebrate celebrar
Cinema cine	Clinic clinica

Grammar Unit 6: Regular Verbs in Spanish

Now I am going to introduce you to verbs in Spanish. Just like in English, we have regular and irregular verbs in Spanish and you will be able to discover the categories they belong to, the variations and conjugations, in order to use them correctly. Keep in mind that because you are learning a complete new language, you will need to practice and study if you wish to master it and a great part of the results will depend on how much time and dedication you devote to this task. I will provide you with a list of the most common verbs as well to make it easier for you to identify them. But, there is also the joy of learning a new element that will further your knowledge of the language and your ability to communicate in a global environment. By the end of this lesson, you will have learned the types of regular verbs in Spanish, their structure, and how to conjugate them in the present indicative. And that is a BIG step.

I will ask you to identify a pattern in these verbs:

Saltar (*To jump)*

Amar (*To love)*

Bailar (*To dance)*

They all share a common ending and different beginnings or stems. In order to learn how to conjugate verbs in Spanish, you will need to identify these two parts of every verb: the stem and the ending. You will perform this division consciously at first and then, with time and practice, it will become natural, just like for every other native speaker.

Here are a few more examples:

Beber (*To drink)*

Saber (*To know)*

Aprender (*To learn)*

Can you identify the common ending? Yes, they all end in –**er**. And there is one more group. Take a look:

Abrir (*To open*)

Partir (*To leave*)

dormir (*To sleep*)

The English equivalent is only there to show you the meaning of the Spanish verb, but they do not necessarily match in terms of regular-irregular verbs. In other words, verbs that are regular in Spanish may be irregular in English and vice versa.

All regular verbs can be put into three categories, depending on their final letters: -**ar** verbs, -**er** verbs and –**ir** verbs. This is the infinitive form of verbs in Spanish.

Now, you will be able to recognize when a verb in Spanish is in the infinitive if it appears with the endings we just saw: -**ar**, -**er** and –**ir**.

To learn how to form sentences, you need to conjugate the verb so that it agrees with the pronoun. In English, the conjugation is rather simple and you only have to learn one variation, but in Spanish you will find a few more forms of the verb, depending on the personal pronoun you use. Let's remember the personal pronouns in Spanish:

Yo (*I*)

Tú (*You*)

Usted (*You -formal-*)

Él / Ella (*He, She*)

Nosotros (*We*)

Vosotros / Ustedes (*You*)

Ellos (*They*)

In Spanish, we can find a difference between you-formal **usted** and you-informal **tú**. There is a coincidence in the conjugation of verbs that agree with the pronoun **Usted** and **Él/Ella**. But we will get back to this later.

Here are some examples of sentences in Spanish. Read them carefully, paying attention to the ending of the verbs.

Verb in Infinitive: Comer /ko-´mer *(to eat)*

Yo com**o** /Yo ´ko-mo *(I eat)*

Tu com**es** /to ´ko-mes *(You eat)*

Él com**e** /Él ´ko-me *(He eat**s**)*

Nosotros com**emos** /no-´so-tros ko´me-mos *(We eat)*

Ustedes com**en** /us-´te-des ´ko-men *(You eat -plural-)*

Ellos com**en** /eyos ´ko-men *(They eat)*

In the classroom, I always ask my students to identify the stem of the verb before moving on to the endings and the conjugation used. In the above sentences, the stem is **com-** and the ending changes according to the personal pronoun used. As we mentioned before, these are called regular verbs because the stem remains the same and the conjugation affects the ending of the words.

I will show you more common verbs and you will be able to find a list of common regular verbs in Spanish in the Vocabulary Section. You will discover that, although at first these variations may seem too difficult to take in, there is a pattern in the variations and you will be able to learn them by practicing. One thing I like to remark when I teach my students this is that each one of us had to do the same practicing when we learned our first words. Your mom and the rest of your family would say a word and you would repeat it, making mistakes, and being corrected by the grown-ups.

Now you have an advantage because you already know how to read and write and as you build your vocabulary, you will have a wide range of words to use in order to make meaningful sentences.

Let's study the pattern I am talking about. The pattern will change depending on the tense. For the Simple Present, you can conjugate the verbs in the following way:

For the subject **yo**, the conjugated form will end with **–o**, leaving the **–ar**, -**er**, -**ir** endings behind:

Yo le**o** (infinitive form: leer – to read) *I read*

Yo habl**o** (infinitive form: hablar – to speak) *I speak*

Yo part**o** (infinitive form: partir – to leave) *I leave*

See how you dropped the infinitive ending to replace it with**–o**? This is true for all regular verbs with this subject in Simple Present.

 Now, the subject **tu** (you, singular, informal) is slightly different. To conjugate verbs with different endings **–ar, er, ir**- you will drop the ending and add **–as**, if it is a verb with **–ar** ending, and **–es** if it is a verb ending with **–er** or **–ir**. Confused? Take a look at the examples to see it clearly:

Infinitive form: saltar *(to jump)* / Tú salt**as** /tu ´sal-tas *(you jump)*

Infinitive form: beber *(to drink)* / Tú beb**es** /tu ´be-bes *(you drink)*

Infinitive form: decidir *(to decide)* / Tú decid**es** /tu de-´ci-des *(you decide)*

In the above examples, the verbs with **–ar** endings change in the present simple to agree with the subject "**tú**" in such a way that**–ar** is dropped and you need to add **–as**.

The verbs with **–er** and **–ir** endings change by dropping**–er** and **–ir** and adding **–es**, in both cases.

Él and **Ella** present similar variations in the present simple. For verbs ending in **–ar**, drop the ending and add **–a**; and for verbs ending in **–er** and **–ir**, drop the final two letters and add **–e**. Here are some examples that my students find useful:

Infinitive: amar *(To love)*

Él am**a** /El ´a-ma *(He loves)* / Ella am**a** /Eya ´a-ma *(She loves)*

Infinitive: saber *(To know)*

Él sabe /El ´sa-be *(He knows)* / Ella sabe /Eya ´sa-be *(She knows)*

Infinitive: vivir *(To live)*

Él vive /El ´vi-ve *(He lives)* / Ella vive /Eya ´vi-ve *(She lives)*

In the above examples, you can see how the –**ar** ending in verbs is replaced by the letter –**a,** and -**er**, -**ir** are replaced by the letter –**e** to conjugate verbs.

I mentioned before that the formal use of **you**, in Spanish **Usted,** matches the subjects **él** and **ella**. These examples show you how verbs are conjugated with the subject Usted.

Infinitive: am**ar** *(To love)* / Usted am**a** /us-´ted ´a-ma *(You love)*

Infinitive: sab**er** *(To know)* / Usted sab**e** /us-´ted ´sa-be *(You know)*

Infinitive: viv**ir** *(To live)* / Usted viv**e** /us-´ted ´vi-ve *(You live)*

As you can see, the conjugated form of the verb in third person (**él, ella**) can be used for the subject **usted**. Knowing how these two coincide will help you in situations where you need to address somebody formally. The form **usted** is preferred when you are not familiar with the person you want to address, in a formal event, when talking to an older person, a boss, a teacher, or when establishing a relationship of respect and hierarchy.

Let's move on to the plural person **nosotros** *(We)*. Read the following sentences and again, identify the verb stem and endings.

Infinitives: am**ar** (To love), sab**er** (To know), viv**ir** (To live)

Nosotros am**amos** /no-´so-tros a-´ma-mos (We love)

Nosotros sab**emos** /no-´so-tros sa-´be-mos (We know)

Nosotros viv**imos** /no-´so-tros vi-´vi-mos (We live)

Sometimes I hear my students complain that there are too many variations. But I like to remind them that learning a new language is a challenge and that they only need to pay attention to each lesson and practice, practice,

practice. In this case, the rule is quite simple: when the subject is **nosotros** *(we)*, simply drop the ending and add –**amos** for verbs ending in –**ar**; -**emos** for verbs ending in –**er**; and –**imos** for verbs ending in –**ir**. The vowel can be used as a cue to know which ending to use. What is more, once you start using this conjugation, you will notice that the ending does bring a sense of closeness, of us being part of a group that performs an action.

I will now teach you how to conjugate verbs for the subject **Ustedes** *(you, plural)*. Before we start with the conjugations, let me explain the difference between **ustedes** and **vosotros**.

In Latin America, the use of **ustedes** is more common and it may be both formal and informal. In an informal situation, somebody may say **ustedes saben bailar** (*You know how to dance)* and then use the same subject in a more formal situation; for example, ustedes redactan las leyes (you write up the laws) to a group of politicians. **Vosotros** is hardly ever used to refer to a plural you in Latin America, but this form is widely used in Spain.

In Spain, the subject **ustedes** is used in formal situations, something similar to a pluralization of the subject usted. **Vosotros**, however, is used as an informal way to address two or more people if you are familiar with them or in a friendly context. The conjugation for the subject **Vosotros** is different from that of the subject ustedes and I will teach you more about it at the end of this chapter. We will focus now on the pronoun **ustedes** and learn how to conjugate verbs for this subject.

Take a look at these examples:

Infinitive verb: mir**ar** – To look / Ustedes mir**an** /us-´te-des ´mi-ran (You look)

Infinitive verb: beb**er** – To drink / Ustedes beb**en** /us-´te-des ´be-ben (You drink)

Infinitive verb: abr**ir** – To open / Ustedes abr**en** /us-´te-des ´a-bren (You open)

Again, there are two variations depending on the verb ending. For –**ar** verbs, drop the ending and add –**an**. For verbs ending in –**er** and –**ir**, drop the last two letters and add –**en**.

Here are a few more similar examples:

Infinitive: sal**ir** (to go out) / Ustedes sal**en** /us-'te-des 'sa-len (You go out)

Infinitive: am**ar** (to love) / Ustedes am**an** /us-'te-des 'a-man (You love)

Infinitive: sab**er** (to know) / Ustedes sab**en** /us-'te-des 'sa-ben (You know)

I will now teach you how to conjugate verbs for the subject **ellos** (*they*). The following verbs will show you the pattern:

Infinitive: mir**ar** (to look) / Ellos mir**an** /'e-yos 'mi-ran (They look)

Infinitive: sab**er** (to know) / Ellos sab**en** /'e-yos 'sa-ben (They know)

Infinitive: sufr**ir** (to suffer) / Ellos sufr**en** /'e-yos 'su-fren (They suffer)

If you look closely, the form of the conjugated verb for the subject **ellos** is the same as the subject **ustedes**.

For verbs ending in **–ar**, drop the ending and add **–an** to the stem. For verbs ending in **–er** and **–ir**, drop the last two letters and add **–en**.

The subject **ellos** and **nosotros** can be used to describe a group made up of masculine elements only or a mixed group of masculine and feminine elements. If you want to talk about a group of people made up of women only, the subject must be adapted to **ellas** *(They – women only)* and **nosotras** *(We – women only).*

At this point, it is important that you read this lesson more than once and start practicing with the model verbs you can find in the vocabulary section. Some of my students often express their concern about so many variations, but with adequate practice, they all master the verb inflections in the end and they can develop real life conversations with native speakers without feeling insecure about the use of verb conjugations. This is the goal of the book, to give you the tools for you to feel comfortable speaking and writing in Spanish - and verb conjugation is a big part of it. So do not waste one minute and start practicing what you just learned!

About the subject Vosotros/Vosotras.

As I previously explained, the form **vosotros/vosotras** is only used in Spain and has some special characteristics. However, you will also be able to identify a pattern just like in the other conjugations. Remember, the use of this form of the subject is not as widely spread as the form **ustedes** and the following examples show the variations:

Infinitive: cant**ar** *(To sing)*

Vosotros cant**áis**

Infinitive: com**er** *(To eat)*

Vosotros com**éis**

Infinitive: sub**ir** *(To go up)*

Vosotros sub**ís**

Notice how the ending –**ar** is dropped and replaced by –**áis**; -**er** is dropped and replaced by –**éis**, and –**ir** is dropped and replaced by –**ís**. The accent is needed there.

Exercises

Exercise 1: Highlight the ending in each of these verbs. Hint: they are all infinitives. You will find the pronunciation between //.

Abrir /a-´brir/ To open

Aprender /a-pren-´der/ To learn

Andar /an-´dar/ To walk

Esperar /es-pe-´rar/ To wait

Recibir /re-si-´bir/ To receive

Partir /par-´tir/ To leave

Pagar /pa -´gar/ To pay

Desear /de-seár/ To wish

Estudiar /es-tu-´diar/ To study

Buscar /bus-´kar/ To search

Caminar /ka-mee-´nar/ To walk

Hablar /a-´blar/ To talk

Vender /ven-´der/ To sell

Vivir /vi-´vir/ To live

Dejar /de-´jar/ To leave

Trabajar /tra-ba-´jar/ To work

Exercise 2: Conjugate the following verbs to make them agree with the subject in the present tense.

Él _____ (asistir)

Yo _____ (escribir)

Nosotras _____ (lavar)

Ella_____ (sufrir)

Ustedes _____ (practicar)

Tú _____ (comer)

Él _____ (alquilar)

Nosotros _____ (discutir)

Ellos _____ (preguntar)

Ellas _____ (comprar)

Tú _____ (bailar)

Yo _____(ganar)

Exercise 3: On a different piece of paper, conjugate the following regular verbs in Spanish for all 6 subjects (yo, tú, él/ella, nosotros, ustedes, ellos). Remember to look the verbs up in the list of regular verbs that appears in the vocabulary section at the end of this book and write down their meaning.

Firmar

Estudiar

Enseñar

Ganar

Buscar

Gastar

Subir

Temer

Caminar

Cocinar

Entrar

Preguntar

Discutir

Beber

Comer

Olvidar

Dejar

Viajar

Exercise 4: Practice the above forms of the subject-verb agreement by providing the correct conjugation for the following verbs:

Hacer

Hablar

Llegar

Comprar

Subir

Leer

Recibir

Entrar

Buscar

Estudiar

Pagar

Amar

Caminar

Describir

At the end of the book, you will find the Unit 6 Key with the correct answers so you can check your progress.

How To Say...

When you need to go somewhere...

¿Puede llevarme a...? /puéde vavme a/

Grammar Unit 7: The Present Tense

The Present indicative in Spanish has a variety of uses, meaning that it comes in handy for different communicative situations. I will teach you how to recognize them and how to be certain about which tense to use. My students find it useful to find the English equivalent, but remember, it is best to relate one tense to a particular situation so you will not force your brain to go through a mental labyrinth every time you create a sentence in Spanish.

In this lesson, I will tell you all about the Present Simple Tense, how to form affirmative, negative, and interrogative sentences, and you will put the conjugations you just learned to good use.

Let's begin with the different uses of the present tense in Spanish:

We use the simple present to talk about a customary action, something you do regularly or repeatedly. For example, the actions you perform every morning, such as waking up, brushing your teeth, drinking coffee, or taking the bus can be expressed using the present simple. Here are a few examples in Spanish:

Yo desayuno a las 7am *(I have breakfast at 7am)*

Yo salgo hacia la oficina a las 8am *(I leave for the office at 8am)*

Yo tomo el autobús a las 8.10 am *(I take the bus at 8.10 am)*

The present simple tense can be used to describe facts such as nature's laws. For example, to describe how something works or an eternal truth. These sentences speak of such facts:

Los pájaros vuelan *(Birds fly)*

El agua es transparente *(Water is transparent)*

You can talk about near future events using the present simple. Especially when describing an immediate and planned action in the future. Here are some examples:

Mañana salgo para Madrid (*Tomorrow I leave for Madrid*)

La fiesta es mañana (*The party is tomorrow*)

El doctor vuelve el lunes (*The doctor returns on Monday*)

Sometimes the Present simple is used to talk about past events to make them appear more recent or to create the feeling of closer action for the audience. This is not very common, but in every case, the context will help you understand that the events are in fact in the past. You can come across this type of usage of the Present Simple in colloquial retellings of past events or in some storytelling. Here are some examples:

El Coronel cena y poco despues empieza la batalla (*The Coronel has dinner and shortly after that, the battle starts*)

Salimos y Pedro dice que no sabe donde están sus llaves (*We got out and Peter says he doesn't know where the keys are*)

As I mentioned before, this usage may show an advanced command of the language because the speaker does not need to make it clear that he is talking about the past, but the context provides that information. When I talk about the context, I am referring to the situation in which the conversation takes place and all other conversations leading to that moment. For example, the first sentence may be said by a teacher at a History class; the second sentence may be uttered by a friend who is talking about the events from last weekend, and so on.

Adverbs and Time Expressions.

One of the elements that will help you recognize the need for a verb in Present Simple is the presence of certain adverbs of time and time expressions that indicate the action or event is happening in any of the four ways I explained to you before. These adverbs are also part of the English language. Think for a moment how you describe your routines or how you talk about facts, how you describe repetitive actions. There are equivalent words and phrases in Spanish and they will become your best friends when it comes to identifying which tense to use, not only in the present simple, but in most tenses.

These are some of the adverbs and time expressions that you may find in sentences in the Present Simple:

Siempre *(Always)*

Todos los días *(Every day)*

Todas las semanas *(Every week)*

Una vez por semana *(Once a week)*

Dos veces por semana *(Twice a week)*

Cada día *(Each day)*

Frecuentemente *(Regularly)*

Seguido, a menudo *(Often)*

Muy seguido *(Very often)*

Normalmente, Generalmente *(Usually)*

A veces *(Sometimes)*

Nunca *(Never)*

Casi nunca *(Hardly ever)*

Verbs and the absence of a subject

You must have noticed that in some of the sample sentences, there was no subject in front of the verb. This is a special feature of the Spanish language. While in English you always need a subject, in Spanish, the characteristics of verbs make it possible to leave the subject out, using only the conjugated verb to make a sentence. How is this possible? Verbs will have different endings according to subject, tense, and even mood (we will get back to this in a more advanced level). With this special feature, you can simply use a conjugated verb and any Spanish speaker will be able to tell which subject and tense you are using. Take a look at the conjugated verb **como** *(I eat).* In that simple word you are conveying the subject **yo** *(I),* the present tense (-**er** ending changes to –**o** in present simple, first person singular), and the indicative mood. This is very common in Spanish and you will get used to discarding the subject when making sentences. But do not worry; we will go step by step until you are confident enough to use a conjugated verb and hiding the subject. These are some samples of regular verbs used without an expressed subject:

(yo) bebo

(tú) nadas

(ellos) viven

(él) paga

Affirmative Sentences in the Simple Present

I get asked a lot by my students about how to form affirmative sentences in the simple present. At this level, you will start by learning how to form simple sentence and as you progress in the study of the language, they will become more complex, even longer with several ideas within one sentence. This is natural and you come across such sentences in English as well. Nevertheless, it is said that in Spanish, sentences tend to be longer and sometimes confusing because of the lack of a subject before a conjugated verb. As I previously mentioned, many sentences can be formed with the conjugated verb only and this is common and grammatically correct. My students often complain that it is hard at first, but then they become used to putting the responsibility of the conjugation on the verb ending and they learn to leave out the subject in order to sound more natural. As I teach you the first steps for making affirmative sentences in Spanish, please keep in mind that not all sentences will display the subject in the form of personal pronouns.

Take a look at the following sentence:

Sofía hace su tarea /so-fía ´a-ce su ta-´re-a/ *(Sofía does her homework)*

In this affirmative sentence, the structure takes the form of:

Subject + conjugated verb + direct object (su tarea). The way to form such sentences is by using the subject (a personal pronoun or a name/object/animal), plus the conjugated verb, plus something else that complements the sentence. It can be an adverb, a direct object, or other function, but in general, it will be something that completes the sense of the sentence.

See? No problem so far and you are already reading full sentences in Spanish. Now let's take this one step further. I have explained how you can leave out the subject. Read the following example:

Leo una revista /léo ´u-na re-´vis-ta (*I am reading a magazine*)

Note: remember that one of the uses of the simple present in Spanish is equivalent to the present progressive or continuous in English.

In this case, the subject is hidden in the verb ending. Because it is an **–er** verb (leer – to read), the ending –o indicates the hidden subject is **Yo** (I). This is how you can start using verbs without a visible subject to make sentences in Spanish.

Here are more examples:

(**nosotros**) Sabemos el alfabeto *(We know the alphabet)*

(**ella/él**) Visita a su abuela *(He/she is visiting his/her grandma)*

(**tú**) Conoces esta ciudad *(You know this city)*

The operation of leaving the subject out is quite common in Spanish and as you go over magazine articles, newspapers or novels, you will come across these types of sentences over and over again. This is why it is important that you learn conjugations so you do not have to stop and think, while you are reading in order to recognize the subject of a verb or how it is conjugated.

Negative Sentences

Forming the negative in Spanish is very simple and that is one of the reasons why my students love this part of the lesson. To make a sentence negative, simply add the word "no" before the conjugated verb. Read the following examples:

Ella no bebe café *(She doesn't drink coffee)*

In the above sentence, you can identify a subject, **ella** (she); the negative word **no**, and the conjugated verb. In Spanish, the verb will still be conjugated after the use of the negative form **no**, whereas in English, you will use the auxiliary **doesn't** and the infinitive verb. This is one difference that my students like to remember because it is fairly simple. After the verb, simply add the rest of the sentence, as we previously mentioned, it could be a direct object, a complement, or an adverb.

These examples will help you identify the negative form:

Nosotros no viajamos en tren *(We do not travel by train)*

El gato no come mucho *(The cat doesn't eat too much)*

Elisa no estudia francés *(Elisa doesn't study French)*

Remember that you can also leave the subject out and place it on the conjugated verb instead:

No sabe jugar *(He/she doesn't know how to play)*

No tememos a los monstruos *(We are not afraid of monsters)*

No hablas italiano *(You don't speak Italian)*

At the end of this lesson, you will find some exercises to help you learn this and identify the subject hidden in the conjugated verb. If you continue to go through each lesson, by the end of the book, you will be able to have a simple conversation in Spanish, read articles on general knowledge, and conjugate verbs properly.

Now let's move on to learn how to formulate questions in Spanish.

Interrogative Sentences

There is really more than one way to formulate a question in Spanish.

Most simple sentences begin with the conjugated verb, plus the subject, plus the rest of the sentence (complement, direct object, adverb, etc.). One example of such structure would be:

¿Ama ella a su novio? (*Does she love her boyfriend?*)

In the above sentence, the conjugated verb **ama** is in first place, then the subject, **ella**, and the rest of the sentence comes next. However, in colloquial speech and in many other medias such as magazine articles, it is acceptable to use the subject at the beginning, place the conjugated verb next, and the rest of the sentence at the end. Here is one example:

¿Ella ama a su novio? (*Does she love her boyfriend?*)

¿Nosotros aprendemos español? (*Are we learning Spanish?*)

¿Ustedes saben manejar? (*Do you know how to drive?*)

This is indeed quite common and you should not worry about using one or the other because both are correct. Just like in the Affirmative and Negative cases, you can leave out the subject in interrogative sentences. The previous examples would look like this:

¿Ama a su novio? (*Does she love her boyfriend?*)

¿Aprendemos Español? (*Are we learning Spanish?*)

¿Saben Manejar? (*Do they know how to drive?*)

Question Words in Spanish

I will now give you a list of question words in Spanish to form what is normally called wh- questions. This list is definitely useful for making questions about time, manner, degree, quantity, and more.

¿Qué? /ke *(What?)*

¿Cómo? /'ko-mo *(How?)*

¿Cuándo? /'kuan-do *(When?)*

¿Dónde? /'don-de *(Where?)*

¿Quién? /ki-'en *(Who?)*

¿Por qué? /por 'ke *(Why)*

These question words go at the beginning of a sentence and when you use them, you must follow the structure: question word + conjugated verb + subject. Take a look:

¿Por qué estudias (tú) Español? *(Why do you study Spanish?)*

¿Donde estudia (ella) Español? *(Where does she study Spanish?)*

Ok, now that you are familiar with these aspects of forming sentences in Simple Present, it is time to practice! Remember, you may not get it right the first time so what will you do? In class, I have an agreement with my students and I want to share it with you. If you get an answer wrong, do not get upset. You are learning a new language and that is an enormous task. Simply check the answer and try to think of where you went wrong, what element caused confusion, and revise that item in the lessons again. Then erase your previous writings and do it all over again, but don't do it immediately, allow a couple of hours or 1-2 days to try again. You will find great advantages in this method and your brain will benefit as well.

So, let's begin practicing!

Exercises

Exercise 1: Put the verbs in brackets in the correct form by conjugating it.

Ella (saber) _____

Nosotros (abrir) _____

Él (comer) _____

Ellos (contestar) _____

Usted (bailar) _____

Tú (aprender) _____

Yo (regresar) _____

Ustedes (ganar) _____

Él (sorprender) _____

Ellos (saludar) _____

Usted (trabajar) _____

Ella (temer) _____

Nosotros (viajar) _____

Tú (olvidar) _____

Yo (nadar) _____

Ustedes (mirar) _____

Exercise 2: Which subject is hidden in the conjugated verb? Revise the rules and check if more than one option is available.

Usamos _____

Tose _____

Llegan _____

Necesito _____

Toca _____

Miras _____

Compran _____

Come _____

Acampamos _____

Admiten _____

Comprendes _____

Acelero _____

Canta _____

Dejas _____

Desayunamos _____

Barren _____

Ayuda _____

Describes _____

Habla _____

Discuten _____

Envías _____

Escuchamos _____

Prepara _____

Rompen _____

At the end of the book, you will find the <u>Unit 7</u> Key with the correct answers so you can check your progress.

Words You Didn't Know You Knew

Culture cultura   Day- día

Decision decisió   Declare declarar

Defense defensa   Delicate delicado

Dentist dentista   Describe describir

Grammar Unit 8: Present Progressive in Spanish

Are you ready for another verb tense? In this lesson, I will teach you how to talk in Spanish about actions in progress. We are going to review and practice the Present Continuous, also called Present Progressive because it is used to describe what is happening at the moment, an action in progress. Now, in order to conjugate verbs in the present continuous, we will take a look at one of the most important verbs in Spanish, the verb **estar**, which is equivalent to the verb "to be."

Altogether, the present progressive is formed by a conjugation of the verb **estar**, plus a present participle and it is equivalent to **be + verb+ing** in English. Because the verb **estar** is irregular, I will first give you details about how to conjugate this verb. These are six simple forms that I ask my students to memorize because they will come in handy for more than one situation, as you will see in the next lesson about the Spanish equivalent of the verb t**o be**.

Conjugation of the verb Estar

Infinitive: Estar /es-´tar *(to be)*

Yo estoy /yo es-´toy *(I am)*

Tú estás /tu es-´tas *(You are)*

Él está /el es-´ta *(He is)*

Ella está /eya es-´ta *(She is)*

Nosotros estamos /no-´so-tros es-´ta-mos *(We are)*

Ustedes están /us-´te-des es-´tan *(You are (plural))*

Ellos están /eyos es-´tan *(They are)*

So, this is the first part of the ingredients to the Present Continuous or Progressive. The verb **estar** serves the purpose of stating a condition, which will be temporary in this tense. The other half of the present progressive is the present participle, which is formed by adding the ending –**ando**, -**endo**, -**iendo** to any verb. Here are some examples:

Hablar – hablando *(Talking)*

Comer – comiendo *(Eating)*

Salir – saliendo *(Going out)*

I am sure you guessed it by now. Yes, there are different conjugations for –ar, -er and –ir verbs. The good news is, you will only need to conjugate the first half, that is, the verb **estar** and then simply use the present particle of a regular or irregular verb with the –**ando**, -**endo**, -**iendo** endings.

Again, you will use different endings whether you are working with an –**ar**, -**er or –ir** verb. But the rule is quite simple. For all –**ar** verbs, drop the ending and add –and**o** to form the continuous participle:

Habl**ar** – habl**ando**

Cant**ar** – cant**ando**

Cocin**ar** – cocin**ando**

By adding the subject and the conjugated verb **estar**, you can form a proper sentence in the present progressive:

Ella está hablando *(She is talking)*

Nosotros estamos cantando *(We are singing)*

Ustedes están cocinando *(You are cooking)*

Remember that in all cases, just like we learned in the previous lessons, you can leave out the subject and use the conjugated verb instead. The conjugation of **estar** gives you every detail you need about the subject, hence this can be hidden.

For verbs ending in –**er** and –**ir**, simply add –**iendo**. Take a look at the following verbs and how you can transform them into present participles.

Correr *(To run)* – corriendo

Beber *(To drink)* – bebiendo

Crecer *(To grow)* – creciendo

Vivir *(To live)* – viviendo

Recibir *(To receive)* – recibiendo

Escribir *(To write)* – escribiendo

Add the conjugated verb **estar** to form sentences in the present progressive:

Estoy viviendo *(I am living)*

Estás escribiendo *(You are writing)*

Está creciendo *(It is growing)*

It is worth mentioning that you will come across some verbs that when conjugated, they take the ending –**yendo**. They have an irregular ending. There are only a bunch of these verbs so I usually ask my students to write a short list with these –**er** and –**ir** verbs. The reason for these **irregular** present participles is that the stem ends in a vowel and leaves the unaccented –i form –**iendo** in the middle. In this case, you will need to replace it with the "Y." Do you think this is too complicated? My students feel the same until they see the following examples:

Caer (*irregular – to fall*): the stem is Ca (-er is the ending), and if you try to replace the ending with –iendo, the weak –i is in the middle of two vowels. So instead you will add -**Y** to the stem and then –endo to form Cayendo.

Leer: the stem is Le (-er is the ending),and again, you will need to replace the –i in –iendo with -**Y** to form the correct spelling: Leyendo.

Oír: the stem is **O** (just one vowel, -ir is the ending, this is an irregular verb) and you will remove the ending, add –**y** and then –**endo** to form oyendo.

Creer: the stem is Cre (-**er** is the ending, this is a regular verb), so you will need to add –**y**, and then –**endo**. The present participle is Creyendo.

Simply put, the following four verbs change to form the present continuous:

Caer – Cayendo

Leer – Leyendo

Oír – Oyendo

Creer - Creyendo

You will have no problem remembering these four words and the irregular verbs are a great introduction to that part of grammar that we will tackle on a different lesson.

Remember that the present progressive is used in Spanish to talk about actions happening at the moment of speaking, especially to talk about interrupted actions, activities, or **what you are doing while you speak**. However, you cannot use the present progressive to talk about future actions like we do in English. Instead you will use the verb **ir + a + infinitive**, where **ir** is conjugated according to the subject. We will get to this later when we discuss the future tense.

All in all, the present progressive or continuous is quite simple and my students love how they can form this tense by using the conjugation of the verb **estar**, plus a present participle. You too will find that with a few simple exercises, you can master this tense in no time. Remember to keep your list of Spanish verbs handy. One trick that my students love is to write in Spanish the verbs you recognize in whatever material you are reading. It can be the newspaper, a novel, or a report for work that you will not have to show to your boss. Anything you can get your hands on. Simply write the Spanish verb, conjugated when possible, above the English word in the text and that will help you get your mind thinking in Spanish, especially if you are bound to review the same text again. And if you cannot write the texts you are reading, you can simplify the task by taking a moment to identify at least one verb in each page, and think of it in Spanish. If you can remember or if you need a hint, you are more than welcome to look at the list of verbs I provided at the end of this book. The only way to finally master the verbs is by repetition and I will share all sorts of tricks to help you repeat the verbs in your mind effortlessly.

Now it's time for some exercises!

Exercises

Exercise 1: Write the correct form of the verb to be in Spanish.

a. Tú _____

b. Él _____

c. Yo _____

d. Ellos _____

e. Nosotros _____

f. Ella _____

g. Juan y Pedro _____

h. Romina y Lucía _____

i. Tomás, Laura y Pedro _____

j. Ustedes _____

Exercise 2: Which subject is hidden in the conjugated verb?

a. Estamos _____

b. Estás _____

c. Está _____

d. Estoy _____

e. Están _____

Exercise 3: Form sentences in the Present Progressive using the given subject and verb, adding the conjugated verb estar and the present participle.

a. Yo – estudiar _____

b. Ella – cocinar _____

c. Tú – viajar _____

d. Él – escribir _____

e. Nosotros – oír _____

f. Ellos – Cantar _____

g. Ellas – Hablar _____

h. Ustedes – beber _____

i. Tú – mirar _____

j. Nosotras – Vivir _____

k. Yo – Creer _____

l. Él – Crecer _____

m. Ella – entrar _____

n. Tú – subir _____

o. Él – sufrir _____

p. Nosotros – trabajar _____

q. Ellos – llegar _____

r. Ellas – diseñar _____

s. Ustedes – caminar _____

t. Tú – andar _____

u. Nosotras – enseñar _____

v. Yo – ganar _____

w. Él – leer _____

At the end of the book, you will find the <u>Unit 8</u> Key with the correct answers so you can check your progress.

Affirmative, Negative, and Interrogative Sentences in the Present Progressive Tense

So far we have studied how to form sentences in the present progressive tense in the affirmative. As you may have noticed, the examples listed above are all affirmative sentences. But what structure should you use when you need to deny something or ask a question? In this part of the lesson, we will take a look at how to form negative and interrogative sentences.

As I mentioned before, the present progressive tense is used in Spanish only to talk about activities or events in progress at the moment of speaking. In affirmative sentences, you will need a subject, then the conjugated form of the verb **estar**, plus the present participle:

Ella está jugando *(She is playing)*

To form negative sentences, simply add the negative **no** before the conjugated verb **estar**:

Ella no está jugando *(She is not playing)*

The negative form *no* comes immediately before the conjugated form of the verb to be, this is especially noticeable when the subject is hidden in the conjugated verb **estar**:

No estamos hablando (*We are not talking*)

In the above example, you can see how the verb **estamos** includes the subject **nosotros** and the negative form **no** comes immediately before, in this case, in the front of the sentence.

To formulate questions in the present progressive, you will use the conjugated verb **estar**, followed by the subject (if visible) and then the present participle. Here are some examples:

¿Están ellos ganando? *(Are they winning?)*

¿Estás tú escribiendo? *(Are you writing?)*

In the above sentences, the estar/subject/present participle rule is applied. However, you can also hide the subject in the conjugated form of the verb **estar**, where the sentence would look like this:

¿Están ganando? *(Are they winning?)*

¿Estás escribiendo? *(Are you writing?)*

Note: In Spanish, you will need to use an opening question mark, in addition to the closing mark. Keep this is mind as it is very important to use the correct punctuation. This is also helpful to identify a question and to give it the right intonation in your speech.

It wasn't so hard, was it? This tense is one of the favorites among my students because it is relatively easy and you can come up with lots of examples from real life. So go ahead and grab your list of verbs. Try to describe what is going on around you. If you can, go to the park or to a cafe and say what other people are doing. It is fun discovering how many verbs you can use with this exercise.

Also, complete the following practice in order to become more confident in your use of the present progressive tense.

Exercises

Exercise 4: Write negative sentences using the cues given.

key.

a. ella – estudiar _____

b. nosotros – cocinar _____

c. ustedes – escribir _____

d. él – cantar _____

e. ellos – protestar _____

f. tú – hablar _____

g. nosotros – vender _____

h. ella – nadar _____

i. tú – buscar _____

j. ellos – oír _____

Exercsie 5: Turn the following sentences into the negative and the interrogative.

Ellas están hablando _____

Estoy regresando _____

Tú estás sufriendo _____

Nosotros estamos comiendo _____

Él está ganando _____

Ellos están cantando _____

Estás caminando _____

Están escuchando _____

Estoy estudiando _____

Estamos practicando _____

Exervise 6: What is wrong with these sentences? Put them into the correct order and make sure the verbs are properly conjugated.

Ella no están cocinando _____

Tú saliendo no estás _____

¿Yo comiendo estamos? _____

Ellos están aprender _____

At the end of the book, you will find the <u>Unit 8</u> Key with the correct answers so you can check your progress.

What To Say...

When you would like them to speak more slowly...

Más despacio por favor /´maspdeio por fávor/

Grammar Unit 9: Ser and Estar, the Verb "To Be" in Spanish

The verbs **Ser** and **Estar** in Spanish may be a little tricky for foreign students who are native speakers of English because both verbs are equivalent to the verb **to be** in terms of usage, but in Spanish they are divided in order to express an **essence** or a **state/condition**. As you did when you studied the "gender" of things in a previous lesson, you will have to learn again how to describe something in terms of its intrinsic characteristics or its temporary condition. A new perspective or paradigm will be put into action here. This is the key to learning the verbs **ser** and **estar** in Spanish, and I will help you become accustomed to using one or the other according to the meaning you want to convey.

Let's talk a little more about the difference between **essence** and **condition** of somebody or something. In Spanish, it is necessary to use a conjugation of the verb **ser** to describe an **essence**, a characteristic that is not temporary, that has been acquired or inherited, and that will be permanent. Some examples of such characteristics are shape, size, color, personality, among others. On the other hand, when we talk about the temporary condition of something, we use the verb **estar** because it will describe a temporary state or condition or because it is not an essential characteristic of that something. As we make progress on this lesson, I will provide you with a list of situations where you will use one verb or the other and this will greatly simplify the thought process.

You are already familiarized with the conjugations of the verb **estar** that we use to form the present progressive tense. Estar is an irregular verb and here is a list of its different conjugations according to the subject:

Yo estoy

Tú estás

Él / Ella está

Eso/ello está

Nosotros estamos

Ustedes están

Ellos están

In order to start forming sentences, you will need to complete the structure of subject and ser/estar with a word or phrase that describes an essence or a condition. I have included useful vocabulary in the vocabulary section of the book that will certainly come in handy for describing anything you want and start practicing the verb to be in Spanish.

The following sentences all describe a condition:

Estoy hambrienta /es-'toi am-bri-'en-ta *(I am hungry)*

Está aburrida /es-'ta a-bu-'rri-da *(She is bored)*

Está nublado /es-'ta nu-'bla-do *(It is cloudy)*

Now, I said before that the verb **ser** is also irregular so I will provide now a list of the conjugations according to each subject. Because it is an irregular verb, you will want to memorize these conjugations. If you are following my advice and keeping a notebook with your doubts, exercises, and personal notes, you may want to write these in a new page to make sure you look at them regularly so you will learn them faster. Here they are:

Yo soy *(I am)*

Tú eres *(You are)*

Él / Ella es *(He/she is)*

Nosotros somos *(We are)*

Ustedes son *(You are)*

Ellos son *(They are)*

The following are all examples of **essential** characteristics so you will need to use the verb **ser**:

Ella es tímida /eya es ´ti-mi-da (*She is shy*)

Nosotros somos latinoamericanos /no-´so-tros ´so-mos la-ti-no-a-me-ri-´ca-nos (*We are Latin American*)

Tú eres inteligente /tu ´e-res in-te-li-´jen-te (*You are intelligent*)

El vaso es alto /el ´va-so es ´al-to (*The glass is tall*)

As you may have noticed, the above characteristics are in fact permanent or essential. They are not bound to change in the near future as a condition or state would.

I usually ask my students to think randomly about examples of characteristics that describe "essence" and "condition" and here is a list I have compiled throughout the years. This is not a comprehensive list, but it will help you get the gist of the difference between the two of them.

Essence:

Alto / tall

Lindo / pretty

Bueno / good

Delicioso / delicious

Cuadrado / square

Prolijo / tidy

Puntual / punctual

Rico / rich

Redondo / round

Nuevo / new

Viejo / old

Moderno / modern

Salado / salty

Honesto / honest

It is up to you now to create your own list. Think of the characteristics that may be permanent or temporary, a state/condition or an essence and add them to the above list until you finish this beginner's course book. It will not only help you memorize the characteristics, but it will also build your vocabulary.

Now it is time to compare both verbs, **ser** and **estar** so you can pinpoint the differences and further your knowledge of the concept.

What is the difference between the following sentences? (Do not worry if you feel at a loss right now, I will explain it to you with plenty of details after this).

Los tomates son caros / Los tomates están caros *(Tomatoes are expensive)*

In English, the sentence is the same so the meaning is taken from the shared context. But, that is not equally necessary in Spanish because the verb is telling you the difference right there. Remember I told you that the verb **ser** conveys a sense of **essence** or permanent state? And then, **estar** conveys a sense of temporary condition, something that may be subjected to change. In the examples I provided, the difference is quite clear:

Los tomates están caros *(tomatoes are expensive)* conveys a temporary characteristic. Maybe you went to the market today and the tomatoes were a little bit overpriced or their tag price is higher than it was before.

Alternatively, if you say Los tomates son caros *(tomatoes are expensive),* it means that they are always more pricey than other products or too pricey for your budget. It is a permanent state or an essential characteristic of tomatoes.

Here is another example. Try to guess it and then I will share some of the comments from my students:

Ella está felíz / Ella es felíz *(she is happy)*

What is the difference between these two? Which one is more permanent? This is yet another case of an adjective that can be used with both meanings –you will see that not all adjectives can be used in this way - and the difference is in the duration of the characteristic.

My students' attempts:

"ella está felíz means that she is happy now because this is the verb we use to form the present progressive so it must be related somehow!"

"ella es felíz is a permanent condition, but it baffles me because happiness is not a permanent state"

Well, both are somewhat right. We do use the verb **estar** to form the present progressive, just like I said at the beginning of our lesson and it is okay if you want to make a relation between the two, but keep in mind that you will also use the verb **estar** for other situations, such as location, weather condition, etc.

The second answer is also correct. It really means that **she is always happy**, in other words, that she is a positive person or that she always finds something to be happy about. Regardless of your acceptance or disagreement with the statement, it conveys a **permanent state** or an essence; therefore, you will need to use the verb **ser**.

Condition

Let's move on to a short list of characteristics that convey a **condition**, as opposed to an essence:

Ocupado / Busy

Molesto / Upset

Contento / Glad

Aburrido* / Bored

Sucio / Dirty

Nublado / Cloudy

Soleado / Sunny

Lluvioso / Rainy (day)

Abierto / Open

Cerrado / Closed

Deprimido / Depressed

Ordenado* / Tidy

Enfermo / Sick

Ansioso / Anxious

In the above list, you will find some verbs marked with an asterisk, which means that depending on the use of ser or estar, the meaning will be different. For example, for the word aburrido (/ah-bu-´rri-do/), it will convey the meaning that somebody is bored or boring. Take a look:

Ella está aburrida *(She is bored)*

Ella es aburrida *(She is boring)*

Notice how **estar** is used to convey a condition, a temporary state, while **es** is used for an essential characteristic.

Uses of Ser

As you may have noticed, I provided examples where the verbs ser and estar were followed by an adjective. However, these verbs are used in a variety of contexts and situations and many times they will be followed by words or phrases other than adjectives; for example - to describe location, profession, origin, and more. I would like to introduce you now to a number of specific usages of the verbs ser and estar, which will certainly come in handy. My students love to learn these uses because they will not have to think hard whether they are talking about a condition or essential characteristic when using these phrases. They are already cooked up for you!

You can use the verb **Ser** to describe a profession or occupation:

Ella es abogada *(She is a lawyer)*

Yo soy estudiante *(I am a student)*

Él es professor *(He is a teacher)*

You can use **Ser** to talk about where someone or something is from: their origin or nationality.

El cuadro es de Italia *(The painting is from Italy)*

Mi abuela es de Portugal *(My Granma is from Portugal)*

Soy de Canadá *(I'm from Canada)*

When talking about the hour, day or date, use Ser

Son las 5.30 pm *(It's 5.30 pm)*

Hoy es jueves *(Today is Thursday)*

Es el 24 de diciembre *(It's December 24th)*

If you want to express someone´s political or religious beliefs and affiliation, use **Ser**:

Ella es católica *(She is a Catholic)*

Ellos son musulmanes *(They are Muslims)*

Él es republicano *(He is a Republican)*

Use **Ser** to express possession, when something belongs to someone.

La casa es de Julia *(It is Julia´s house)*

El anillo es de Ana *(It's Ana´s ring)*

Los libros son de Jorge *(The books are George's)*

To describe what something is made of, use Ser:

La mesa es de Madera *(The table is made of wood)*

La muñeca es de plastico *(The doll is made of plastic)*

Ser is used with adjectives to describe certain characteristics, especially inherent or essential ones:

Ella es honesta *(She is an honest person)*

Ellos son atléticos *(They are athletic)*

El niño es alto *(The kid is tall)*

You can use the verb **Ser** to describe family and other relationships:

Ella es mi amiga *(She is my friend)*

Juan es hermano de Laura *(Juan is Laura's brother)*

Ella es mi tía *(She is my aunt)*

You can also use the verb **Ser** to describe where something is taking place, especially for events:

La reunión es en la oficina *(The meeting is at the office)*

La fiesta es en mi casa *(The party is at my house)*

Some impersonal constructions will take the verb **Ser**. Here are some examples:

Es necesario *(It is necessary)*

Es esencial *(It is essential)*

Es importante *(It is important)*

Uses of Estar

I will now teach you the uses of our other favorite verb: **Estar**. If you are anything like my students, you will find this list really helpful!

When you need to describe where something is located (physically or geographically) you need to use **Estar**:

Ella está en Chile *(She is in Chile)*

La nueva mesa está en la sala *(The new table is in the living room)*

Estoy en la oficina *(I am at the office)*

Estar is used in certain expressions and idioms. There are a few, so I will share some of them with you:

Estar de viaje *(To be travelling / to be on a trip)*

Estar de acuerdo *(To agree)*

Estar de vuelta *(To be back)*

Estar en la ruina *(To be broke)*

Estar de moda *(To be in fashion / to be fashionable)*

This one you already know: to describe a temporary state or condition, you use **Estar** plus an adjective

Ella está enojada *(She is upset)*

La bebida está fría *(The beverage is cold)*

Está nublado *(It is cloudy)*

Finally, **Estar** is also used with a present participle (verbs with **–ando**, **-endo**, **-iendo** endings) to form the present progressive tense, as I explained in a previous lesson:

Ella está estudiando *(She is studying)*

Estamos hablando *(We are talking)*

Están llegando (*They are coming)*

Ser and Estar in Affirmative, Negative, and Interrogative sentences

It is time now to talk about how to make negative and interrogative sentences with the verbs **Ser** and **Estar**. You may have noticed that all the examples I have provided so far are affirmative sentences. Let me now explain to you how to structure all three forms, where to place the verbs, and more. Let's go!

Affirmative sentences

Ser and **Estar** are both verbs, irregular verbs; to form affirmative sentences, you need to follow the rules of the present simple (I will describe later how to use these verbs in the past and future tenses).

Here are some examples:

Ella está en Holanda *(She is in the Netherlands)*

Mike está ocupado *(Mike is busy)*

In the above examples, you needed to use a subject plus the verb **estar** to describe something about that subject. This is the common structure that you will use with the verb **estar**.

Remember that you can always hide the subject within the verb, in this case, **estar**:

(Ella) está en Holanda; (Mike) está ocupado

The same structure is used for the verb **Ser**:

Yo soy *profesora (I am a teacher)*

Nosotros somos de Alemania *(We are from Germany)*

Similarly to the verb **Estar**, you can say what or how a subject is by using the verb **ser**. You can form statements by using a subject plus the verb **ser**:

Ella es amable *(She is kind)*

Negative Sentences

To form negative sentences, I will again ask you to remember the rules for the simple present tense. Take a look at the examples:

Ella no está enferma *(She is not sick)*

Ellos no están en la ciudad *(They are not in the city)*

The negative form **no** will be placed immediately before the conjugated verb Estar. Here are some examples with the verb **Ser**:

Yo no soy abogada *(I am not a lawyer)*

Usted no es de aquí *(You are not from here)*

Again, the word **no** goes immediately before the conjugated verb **Ser**. In both cases –for **Ser** and **Estar** verbs- you can hide the subject in the verbs. Here are the same negative sentences with a hidden subject:

No está enferma *(She is not sick)*

No están en la ciudad *(They are not in the city)*

No soy abogada *(I am not a lawyer)*

No es de aquí *(You are not from here)*

My students often ask me if this is the only way to make a negative statement in Spanish and the answer is no. You can also use words such as:

Jamás *(never)*

Nunca *(never)*

de ninguna manera *(in no way)*

See the above words and phrases in the following examples:

Ella jamás está feliz *(She is never happy)*

Nosotros nunca somos puntuales *(We are never punctual)*

Interrogative Sentences

Interrogative sentences can take many forms in Spanish. This is sometimes confusing for students, but in fact it gives you a little bit of freedom when making interrogative sentences. The truth is that you will hear many different structures for questions. Take a look at these examples:

¿Es esta tu casa? (*Is this your house?*)

¿Esta es tu casa? (*Is this your house?*)

¿Tu casa es esta? (*Is this your house?*)

All three forms are equally correct and some native speakers may argue that the first one is quite formal, while the last option is the most informal structure.

I recommend that you use the most common structure until you are comfortable enough to use either one of the three. In any case, it is important that you can recognize all the options for making an interrogative sentence.

Most commonly used:

¿ + verb Ser/Estar + subject + rest of the sentence + ?

Notice that it is important to place an inverted question mark at the beginning of the sentence. This is a distinctive characteristic of the Spanish language so your writing will only be correct if you use both question marks when asking a question.

Exercises

Exercise 1: Say whether the speaker describes an essence or condition.

Estoy aburrida _____

Ella es inteligente _____

Somos hermanos _____

Estamos cansados _____

Ellos están arriba _____

Es muy bella _____

La fiesta es en su casa _____

Está nublado _____

Es moderna _____

Está enferma _____

Exercise 2: Turn the following sentences into negative and interrogative

La niña es tímida _____

Estamos en la oficina _____

Ella es alta _____

Él es médico _____

Ellos están hambrientos _____

Está nublado _____

El niño está aquí _____

Yo soy la hija de Laura _____

El pastel es delicioso _____

La habitación está desordenada _____

Exercise 3: Which verb or verbs would you use with these words (ser/estar)?

Soleado _____

Católico _____

Aburrido _____

Contento _____

Hablando _____

Carpintero _____

Doctora _____

Tu padre _____

En Chile _____

Moderno _____

Nuevo _____

Desordenado _____

Deprimido _____

Las 3.15am _____

De madera _____

Italiano _____

Exercise 4: There is something wrong with these words. Read them carefully and correct the mistakes.

La flor está rosa _____

El cuadro está moderno _____

Están las 4.10pm _____

Somos deprimidos _____

Somos en Argentina _____

Ellos están profesores _____

El niño es en la habitación _____

La mesa está cuadrada _____

Ella está mi madre _____

No somos cansados _____

At the end of the book, you will find the Unit 9 Key with the correct answers so you can check your progress.

Words You Didn't Know Knew You		
Elephant elefante	Energy energía	Example ejemplo
Exam examen	Excuse excusa	Explore explorar
Extreme extremo	Familiar familiar	Family familia

Grammar Unit 10: Possessive Adjectives

Ok, you may have identified some possessive adjectives in the previous lessons. I am talking about those little words that can do so much for us as students and can open up a new world of relationships between elements. Possessive adjectives are used to describe who the owner of something is. Take a look at the following examples:

Esta es mi silla (*This is my chair*)

Él es mi padre (*He is my father*)

Esta es su casa (*This is his/her/their house*)

Él es tu amigo (*He is your friend*)

In the above examples, you can identify different words that I used to describe a relationship between two elements; for example, the chair and me. In Spanish, there are different forms of possessive adjectives, depending on the subject. But first, let me remind you what possessive adjectives are:

My – Your – His – Her – Its – Our – Their

In Spanish you will need to use the following forms of the possessive adjectives:

Yo – Mi

Tú – Tu*

Él - Su

Ella – Su

Nosotros – Nuestro/a/os/as

Ustedes - Su

Ellos – Su

*Notice that when you use the form **Tú** (you), it takes a written accent, while **Tu** (your) does not. This is an important difference and a good way to introduce you to the rules of accentuation, but do not worry about them just yet, simply remember that when you are talking to somebody in particular, you want to "stress" that it is Tú and nobody else…

As you can see in the list I presented, there are 4 main forms of the possessive adjectives in Spanish: Mi – Tu – Su – Nuestro.

There is also the form **Vuestro**, which is used for the subject **Vosotros**. As I mentioned at the beginning of this course, we will be focusing on LatinAmerican Spanish, as opposed to European Spanish. The form Vosotros and its possessive adjective Vuestro is used almost exclusively in Spain, hence we will only recognize its usage, but will not dwell on it.

Now take a look at these new examples:

Estos son mis lápices (*These are my pencils*)

Ellas son mis amigas (*They are my friends*)

Son nuestras fotos (*These are our pictures*)

Son tus perros (*They are your dogs*)

After years of teaching, I have found that students always have issues with this rule, maybe simply because it is completely opposite to English. I will try to put it in simple words so you can get it from the beginning without any hassles:

In Spanish, possessive adjectives agree with the nouns they modify, not the subject. In other words, if the noun after the possessive adjective is plural, it will take a plural possessive adjective. These are the two forms of mi – tu – and su:

Singular noun: mi

Plural noun: mis

Singular noun: tu

Plural noun: tus

Singular noun: su

Plural noun: sus

It looks quite simple, but my students often make the following mistakes:

Estas son **su** medias (*These are his socks*)

Mis padres rentan **sus** casa (*My parents rent their house*)

Ella lee **su** libros (*She reads her books*)

Reflect on the above examples and try to discover why they make these mistakes. Is it because they are trying to make the possessive adjective agree with the subject? If so, remember the rule: the possessive adjectives match the noun, not the subject. It is all about the noun!

Mi – Tu and Su only have two forms, for singular and plural nouns, but the other possessive adjective – nuestro — has four variations, depending not only in the number of nouns it modifies, but also on the gender of nouns.

In this way, **nuestro** can take the following forms:

Nuestro (singular, masculine noun)

Nuestra (singular, feminine noun)

Nuestros (plural, masculine noun)

Nuestras (plural, feminine noun)

Here are some examples:

Este es nuestro perro

Estos son nuestros perros

Esta es nuestra hija

Estas son nuestras hijas

Remember that, in Spanish, noun gender is an important part of the language and this is another step you are taking to master this difficult concept. If you need to revise noun gender, go back to the lesson on this book that explains all about it.

A special note about Su

In the above list, you will find that **Su** appears for many different subjects, both singular and plural; for example: **su (de él); su (de ella); su (de ellos); su (de usted).** Take a look at how you can use this possessive adjective:

Laura habla con **su** amiga. (*Laura is talking with her friend.*)

Pedro habla con **su** amigo. (*Pedro is talking with his friend.*)

Usted habla con **su** madre. (*You (formal) are talking with your mother.*)

Ellos hablan con **su** profesora. (*They are talking with their teacher.*)

But what happens in the following example:

Laura y Pedro hablan con su amiga.

Are they talking to Laura's or Pedro's friend? Or is it a friend of both? Sometimes this information can be found in the context. For example, if you see a movie or a real life situation, it might be quite clear who that **su** refers to. But in most cases, it may be necessary to add more information. Even in spoken Spanish, it is not rare to hear somebody ask for clarification, as in "whose friend?, Laura's or Pedros'?", and this is true also for native speakers.

For this lesson, I will ask you to read the key parts and study them for 20 minutes before completing the exercises. And remember, focus on the differences and try to think of a mental image when possible to help you remember the rules. Then, practice!

Exercises

Exercise 1: Write the correct possessive adjective.

Tú _____

Yo _____

Ella _____

Nosotros _____

Ellos _____

Ustedes _____

Usted _____

Él _____

Exercise 2: Use the correct possessive adjective according to the subject and noun combination.

Yo – libros _____

Tu – casa _____

Él – novia _____

Ella – padres _____

Nosotros – llaves _____

Usted – teléfono _____

Ellos – documentos _____

At the end of the book, you will find the Unit 10 Key with the correct answers so you can check your progress.

What To Say...

When asking for the bill at a restaurant...

¿Podría traerme la cuenta por favor?

Grammar Unit 11: The Future Simple Tense

You have already learned how to talk about routines, customary actions, and actions in progress when I explained the simple present and present progressive tenses. Now it is time to expand your knowledge and take it one step forward – I will teach you all about the future tense and how to describe future actions and events.

Now, this tense is quite popular among my students because it is really easy to learn, there are few variations and they are easy to conjugate. But first, let's take a look at the uses of the future tense in Spanish.

You will find there are three primary uses for the future tense:

To talk about future actions and events: in this case, the use of the future is similar to that of the auxiliary **will** in English. Here is an example:

Pediré pastas (*I will order pasta*)

You can also use the future tense in Spanish to make assumptions: this can be a little confusing because in this case, you will use the future form of the verb to make assumptions or to indicate the probability of something happening in the present. This is a common use in Spanish, see the following example: el sabrá la verdad – he must know the truth/he probably knows the truth. As you can see in the previous example, the verb used is in the future, but the assumption is made about the present or a present action. In most cases, the ambiguity disappears when you use the context to understand the meaning of the sentence.

The third use of the future tense is not as common as the previous two, but still worth mentioning: emphatic commands. If you want to convey a strong demand, use the future tense: estudiarás toda la noche – You WILL study all night; tomarás el autobús – you WILL take the bus.

Now it is a good time to talk about conjugations in the future tense and this is something that my students love to hear: there are few variations in terms of what ending to use to form the future. Take a look at the following examples:

Verb: estudiar (infinitive form)

Yo estudiar**é**

Tú estudiar**ás**

Él estudiar**á**

Nosotros estudiar**emos**

Ustedes estudiar**án**

Ellos estudiar**án**

As you can see in the above examples, there are only 5 different endings (leaving out the ending –éis, used only in Castilian Spanish) and they are:

-**é** for the subject *yo*

-**ás** for the subject *tú*

-**á** for the subjects él and *ella*

-**emos** for the subject *nosotros*, and

-**án** for the subjects ustedes and *ellos*

Remember also that the form usted (you – formal) takes the same ending as **él** and **ella**, so:

-**á** for the subject usted

Also, you can use the feminine form for two of the subjects: **nosotras** and **ellas**.

Notice that all of the endings, except the one for the subject **nosotros**, take a written accent. Remember to include it in your writings to avoid a spelling mistake.

Now that you can recognize the endings, let's talk about the stem. In the previous tenses, you needed to identify the stem in order to add the ending, but this case is different and I should add, easier. You will simply need to use the infinitive of each verb and add the ending as described above. Also, you do not need to decide whether it is an **–ar**, **-er** or **–ir** verb because all three take the same endings, you will only need to decide which ending to use in order to make it agree with the subject:

Infinitive: Adorar *(to adore)*

Yo adorar**é** (*I will adore*)

Tú adorar**ás** (*You will adore*)

Él adorar**á** (*He will adore*)

Nosotros adorar**emos** (*We will adore*)

Ustedes adorar**án** (*You will adore*)

Ellos adorar**án** (*They will adore*)

See how the infinitive verb remains the same and then you simply add the ending according to the subject? Now let's study an **–er** verb:

Infinitive: Creer *(to believe)*

Yo creer**é** (*I will believe*)

Tú creer**ás** (*You will believe*)

Él creer**á** (*He will believe*)

Nosotros creer**emos** (*We will believe*)

Ustedes creer**án** (*You will believe*)

Ellos creer**án** (*They will believe*)

Now, let's complete the series with one example of an **–ir** verb:

Infinitive: Vivir *(to live)*

Yo vivir**é** (*I will live*)

Tú vivir**ás** (*You will live*)

Él vivir**á** (*He will live*)

Nosotros vivi**remos** (*We will live*)

Ustedes vivir**án** (*You will live*)

Ellos vivir**án** (*They will live*)

As with other tenses, you can omit the subject and use the conjugated verb alone to convey the same meaning; that is, hiding the subject in the conjugated verb. With the above examples in mind, they would look like this: viviré, vivirás, vivirá, viviremos, vivirán.

So far we have studied the affirmative form of the future tense. Here is the structure that you need to use in detail:

Subject + conjugated verb in the future + rest of the sentence

I will now teach you how to form negative and interrogative sentences in the future tense, in Spanish.

Negative sentences

The Spanish language is quite straight forward in forming negative sentences, one feature that my students are certainly thankful for! You can simply add the word **no** between the subject and the conjugated verb or directly before the conjugated verb in more complex sentences. See this example:

Ella no estudiará (*She will not study*)

Notice how the verb keeps the ending the same, that is, infinitive + -á to agree with the subject and the word **no** is placed immediately before. Here are some more examples:

Él no dormirá (*He will not sleep*)

Nosotros no iremos (*We will not go*)

Tú no hablarás (*You will not speak*)

Ellos no viajarán (*They will not travel*)

Remember that the subject and the conjugated verb must agree. You can also leave the subject out or in other words, hide it in the conjugated verb and the message stays the same.

Interrogative sentences

I mentioned before that the Spanish language is quite flexible when it comes to forming questions and you can typically ask something in three ways:

¿Dormirá ella aquí? *(Will she sleep here?)*

¿Ella dormirá aquí? *(Will she sleep here?)*

¿Aquí dormirá ella? *(Will she sleep here?)*

All three structures are correct and in colloquial use the second option is probably the most popular. But normally, you will want to reverse the order of subject and verb:

¿ + conjugated verb + subject + object + ?

Eg. ¿Estará ella en la ciudad?

Remember to include an opening question mark at the beginning of the sentence. Also, intonation is definitely important because some people will not reverse the order of subject and verb and will rely only on intonation to imply a question, as opposed to a statement.

Now that you have learned how to talk about the future in Spanish, make questions and negative statements, study the lesson for 45 minutes before going on to the exercises.

Exercises

Exercise 1: Write the following verbs in the correct form in the Future Tense.

Yo (asistir) _____

Ustedes (esperar) _____

Ellos (alquilar) _____

Ella (entrar) _____

Tú (buscar) _____

Él (beber) _____

Nosotros (preparar) _____

Yo (enseñar) _____

Ustedes (preguntar) _____

Ellos (firmar) _____

Ella (caminar) _____

Tú (comer) _____

Él (olvidar) _____

Nosotros (tomar) _____

Yo (leer) _____

Ustedes (mandar) _____

Ellos (bailar) _____

Nosotros (ganar) _____

Yo (escribir) _____

Ustedes (creer) _____

Ella (tocar) _____

Tú (viajar) _____

Él (comprender) _____

Ella (regresar) _____

Tú (subir) _____

Él (cocinar) _____

Nosotros (llegar) _____

Yo (vender) _____

Tú (cubrir) _____

Ellos (sonreír) _____

Exercise 2: Turn the following sentences into negative and interrogative

Ella llegará mañana _____

Nosotros seremos abuelos _____

Él vivirá aquí _____

Ella viajará el sábado _____

Tú visitarás la ciudad _____

Ellos estarán contentos _____

Ustedes jugarán mañana _____

Ella comprará comida _____

Exercise 3: The following sentences describe what Sam and Vane will do when they arrive to the city next week. But the sentences are incorrect. Find the errors and correct them.

Sam y Vane estarás en la ciudad la próxima semana.

_____

Ellos visitarás el museo.

_____

Vane comprarán en las tiendas.

_____

Sam caminaremos por el pueblo

_____

Ellos bailaremos en una disco

_____

Ellos no mirarás una película

_____

Sam y Vane alquilaré un auto

_____

At the end of the book, you will find the Unit 11 Key with the correct answers so you can check your progress.

Words You Didn't Know You Knew

Fruit- fruta	Future- futuro	Gallery- galería
General- general	Goal- gol	Habit- hábito
Hamburger- hamburguesa	History- historia	Horoscope- horóscopo

Grammar Unit 12: More about the Future Tense

You have just finished learning one way of talking about the future, but this is not the only one there is. In this lesson, I will teach you how to talk about future actions and events using other forms of the future tense. Why is this important? The Spanish language offers a variety that is worth learning because in most informal situations, you will come across other ways of using the future tense, as well as other tenses that we have discussed. You need to be able to understand them in the first stages of your learning process and eventually use these tenses just like the native speakers of Spanish do.

These other ways of expressing the future are really common, and you will be happy to hear that they are quite easy to learn!

First, let's talk about an old friend of ours: the present tense. Yes, the present tense can be used to talk about future actions and events, especially in informal or colloquial expressions. Take a look at these examples:

Juana llega el martes *(Juana will arrive on Tuesday)*

Hablamos mañana *(We will talk tomorrow)*

This is one of the uses we discussed when I taught you all about the simple present. While the verb is in the present, the event to which it refers is in the future. So, how can you recognize when a speaker is using the present tense to refer to the present or to the future? Pay attention to the adverbs of time and time expressions that may appear. You will find a list of time expressions later in this lesson. If the sentence does not contain a time expression, you can obtain this information from the context. For example, are you talking about future plans or current events? Is the speaker describing what they plan to do or talking about a present situation? Are there any other indicators in the previous sentences? These are the hints you will get in a conversation or text when there is no time expression to count on.

Remember the conjugation of the simple present, used here to express the future:

Verb in Infinitive: Comer /ko-´mer *(To eat)*

Yo com**o** /yo ´ko-mo *(I eat)*

Tu com**es** /tu ´ko-mes *(You eat)*

Él com**e** /Él ´ko-me *(He eats)*

Nosotros com**emos** /no-´so-tros ko-´me-mos *(We eat)*

Ustedes com**en** /us-´te-des ´ko-men *(You eat)*

Ellos com**en** /eyos ´ko-men *(They eat)*

In other words, you will drop the –ar, -er, and –ir endings and add:

Yo -**o**

Tú -**es**

Él/Ella -**e**

Nosotros -**emos**

Ustedes -**en**

Ellos -**en**

You can use the present tense especially to talk about future events that are happening in the near future; for example, within the next couple of hours or the next couple of days.

Ir a +Infinitive: Another way of talking about the future

This is perhaps the most common way of talking about the future and in many cases, the preferred way for native Spanish speakers, especially in colloquial conversations. For foreign learners, it has the advantage of being extremely easy to learn, something that my students really appreciate and in many cases, they prefer to use this instead of the simple future that I taught you in a previous lesson.

You can identify it as an equivalent of the English form **going to + infinitive** and it is used in the same situations: for actions and events in the future. Because in Spanish it includes an irregular verb in its structure, I will first teach you how to conjugate this verb. Then I will provide examples so you can see how easy it really is and will start loving it like my other students!

Conjugation of **Ir** (to go)

Yo voy

Tú vas

Él va

Nosotros vamos

Ustedes van

Ellos van

Remember that you also need the preposition **a**, that is, the conjugated verb Ir + a + another verb in infinitive (with –**ar**, -**er** and –**ir** endings). Here are some examples:

Yo voy a beber café (*I'm going to drink coffee*)

Vamos a visitar la ciudad (*We are going to visit the city*)

Alejandra va a estudiar mañana (*Alejandra is going to study tomorrow*)

So, as you can see in the above examples, you can use the Ir a + infinitive to talk about future actions, especially those that you have planned in advance.

You will need to use any regular or irregular verb (-**ar**, -**er** and –**ir**) with the Ir a + infinitive. And I mentioned that this tense is definitely easy to learn because you do not need to make any changes to the second verb at all, you simply need to remember the conjugation of Ir for each subject in order to use this structure to talk about the future. Remember, it's voy – vas – va – vamos – van – van

Vamos a cantar (*We are going to sing*)

Van a cocinar pizza (*They are going to make pizza*)

Voy a regresar temprano (*I'm going to be back early*)

Ella va a caminar por la playa (*She is going to walk along the beach*)

Ustedes van a ganar (*You are going to win*)

Negative and Interrogative sentences

Just like with the other tenses I have taught you, you will be able to form the negative using the word **no**, but the question is, where should you place it? Because you have two verbs, it may be a little confusing. Here is the answer to your question:

Ella no va a cantar (*She is not going to sing*)

Nosotros no vamos a cocinar (*We are not going to cook*)

Yes, that is correct; the word "no" for negation goes immediately before the conjugated verb **ir**. The rest of the verbs stay the same, the conjugated verb **ir** and the infinitive are not affected and no new variations are needed.

Now, I will teach you how to ask questions using this structure. Remember how you normally need to invert the order of verbs? The Spanish language allows for some flexibility when forming questions and you will come across different ways of ordering the words in a sentence. Here is one example:

¿Va a asistir ella a la fiesta? (*Is she going to attend the party?*)

¿Ella va a asistir a la fiesta? (*Is she going to attend the party?*)

¿Va ella a asistir a la fiesta? (*Is she going to attend the party?*)

The three possible variations are:

¿+ ir (conjugated) a + infinitive (-ar, -er, -ir) + subject +?

¿Va a asistir ella a la fiesta?

¿+ subject + ir (conjugated) a + infinitive

¿Ella va a asistir a la fiesta?

¿+ ir (conjugated) + subject + a + infinitive +

¿Va ella a asistir a la fiesta?

The last one is probably the least used form of asking questions, but it can easily become more common if you simply omit the subject and hide it in the conjugated verb. In that case, the sentence would look like this:

¿Va a asistir a la fiesta? – Where the subject (she) is implied or hidden.

In other words, if you prefer to omit naming the subject by hiding it in the conjugated verb, you will discover that all sentences look the same:

¿Va a asistir (ella) a la fiesta?

¿(Ella) va a asistir a la fiesta?

¿Va (ella) a asistir a la fiesta?

Is she going to attend the party?

Remember that this is possible only under certain circumstances, where the subject is clear for both the speaker and the person who receives the message.

Adverbs of time and time expressions

As with other tenses, I will teach you some of the most commonly used adverbs of time and time expressions that will help you not only identify a sentence in the future tense, but also make your own statements. These time expressions can be used with all of the forms of the future tense that I have taught you so far: Simple future and **Ir** a + infinitive.

Después (Later)

Luego (Later)

Pronto (Soon)

Mañana (Tomorrow)

Esta noche (Tonight)

El próximo sábado (Next Saturday)

"El próximo/la próxima" (next) works for days of the week, months and years:

El próximo mes (Next month)

La próxima semana (Next week)

El próximo año (Next year)

El año que viene (Next year)

Remember that you can always hide the subject in the conjugated verb like we did in some of the previous examples.

Now that you have learned all the basics about the future tense, it is time to study and practice. You have gone through this lesson and now I will ask you to study the concepts again for 45 minutes. Think of the complications you may find and any other questions that arise when you read the examples and look for the answers in the text. After giving your brain 45 minutes to incorporate this new knowledge, grab a pencil or pen and start working on the exercises!

Exercises

Exercise 1: Use the cues to form a sentence in the future tense using the simple present. Add an adverb of time or time expression from the lesson.

Lucía / llegar _____

El atleta / correr _____

Yo / viajar _____

La artista / cantar _____

Nosotros / viajar _____

Su novio / regresar _____

Yo / cocino la cena _____

El actor / firmar autógrafos _____

Los novios / viajar _____

La tienda / abrir _____

El tren / salir _____

Exercise 2: Write sentences using the following verbs in "Ir a + infinitive" form of the future tense.

Laura / acampar en el bosque _____

María / cocinar la cena _____

El doctor / escribir una nota _____

Nosotros / viajar a Londres _____

Ellos / ganar la final _____

Tú / comprar un presente _____

Juan y Pedro / aprender francés _____

Yo / pagar la cuenta _____

La profesora / preparar la lección _____

El niño / romper el vaso _____

Los hombres / trabajar _____

Mi abuela / cocinar una torta _____

At the end of the book, you will find the Unit 12 Key with the correct answers so you can check your progress.

Words You Didn't Know

Identity- identidad	Idiot- idiota	Image- imagen
Impossible- imposible	Incomplete- incompleto	Incorrect- incorrecto
Insect- insecto	Intelligent- inteligente	Justice- justicia

Grammar Unit 13: The Past Simple Tense: Preterite

So far you have learned how to talk about events and activities in the present and the future with variations for the two of them. Another important pillar of basic understanding in the Spanish language is a good command of the Past Tense(s). Now, I will tell you that similarly to the English tense(s), there are many structures for Spanish, depending on the meaning you want to convey.

To start with the Past Tense(s), I will teach you everything about the Preterite, one tense that my students love because it is quite simple to understand, and you can use it to retell most past events and activities.

I will start by mentioning that there are two past tenses that are, let's say, in the same level when it comes to describing the past, but they do so from different perspectives. They take different endings, and their meaning slightly differs one from the other. One of these tenses is the preterite and the other one is the imperfect. Now, my students usually find them confusing, but the purpose of this book is to make it simple for you to notice the differences and to learn to use them properly. Having said that, let's begin learning how to conjugate verbs in the preterite.

Most verbs, whether regular or irregular, can be put into the preterite. This tense is used to describe past events that have a definite beginning and end. These actions are considered completed and the time of beginning and end may or may not be stated in the sentence. Take a look at the following example of a verb conjugated in the preterite (look up the verb in your list of regular verbs at the end of this book to remember the meaning, if you haven't yet):

Verb: Cantar /kan-´tar/

Yo canté

Tu castaste

Él cantó

Nosotros cantamos

Ustedes cantaron

Ellos cantaron

Notice how the stem or root of the regular verb stays the same, while the ending changes according to the subject.

Now, you will find that regular –ar verbs and regular –er and –ir verbs take different endings. But don't worry, there are only two variations, one for –ar verbs, and one for –er and –ir verbs. To conjugate a regular –ar verb in the preterite, drop the -ar and add the following endings according to each subject:

-é for the subject yo

-aste for the subject tú

-ó for the subjects él or ella

-amos for the subject nosotros

-aron for the subject ustedes

-aron for the subject ellos

So, with this in mind, the conjugation of a regular –ar verb such as amar (to love) looks as follows:

Yo amé *(I loved)*

Tu amaste *(You loved)*

Él / ella amó *(He/she loved)*

Nosotros amamos *(We loved)*

Ustedes amaron *(You loved)*

Ellos amaron *(They loved)*

Remember that you can always leave the subject out and simply hide it in the conjugation, that is, using the conjugated verb will give you the exact indication of which subject it is you are talking about. When the context does not provide such information, then you can add the subject as a way to clarify the message.

Also, do not forget to use the written accent mark where appropriate.

Now, do you know how regular –er and –ir verbs always seem to go hand in hand when it comes to conjugation? Well, this case is not different and both categories of verbs will take the following endings, according to each subject:

-í for the subject yo

-iste for the subject tú

-ió for the subjects él or ella

-imos for the subject nosotros

-ieron for the subject ustedes

-ieron for the subject ellos

Read the following examples for **–er** and **–ir** verbs (and look up their meaning in your list of verbs at the end of this book if you don't remember):

Correr /ko-´rrer/

Yo corrí

Tú corriste

Él / ella corrió

Nosotros corrimos

Ustedes corrieron

Ellos corrieron

Again, notice how the stem of the regular verb stays the same. Here are some examples for an **–ir** verb:

Verb: Salir /sa-´lir/ *(to go out)*

Yo salí

Tú saliste

Él/ella salió

Nosotros salimos

Ustedes salieron

Ellos salieron

There is one common mistake that even some native Speakers make, which is to add an –**s** to the ending –**iste** in the second person singular (**tú**). This is in fact a sign of poor education and a lexical error and you should definitely avoid it, even if you hear it from some speakers, as this is not the correct form. Remember, the subject **Tú** is singular and never takes an s at the ending.

Now that you know how to conjugate a lot of regular verbs in the preterite, let's take a look at the uses of this Past Tense.

Uses of the Preterite

As a general rule, I taught you that the preterite is used for actions and events in the past that are seen as completed with a definite beginning and a definite ending, whether it is stated or not. Now I will give you more details regarding what type of events and activities you can talk about using the preterite:

Use the Preterite for single events in the past with a definite beginning and a definite ending (stated or not)

Ella cocinó una torta anoche *(She made a cake last night)*

Nosotros compramos una botella de vino *(We bought a bottle of wine)*

As you can see in the above examples, the events are individual actions with a beginning and an ending. To cook or to buy something are single actions, meaning that they have a definite duration.

Use the preterite to describe a series of actions or events in the past, as in a chain of events or consecutive actions.

Él compró la casa, la reparó y la vendió. *(He bought the house, repaired it and sold it.)*

Use the preterite to describe actions that were repeated a specific number of times or for events and actions that took place during a particular period.

Trabajó allí por 2 años *(He worked there for 2 years)*

Ella cantó tres canciones *(She sang three songs)*

Notice that when you talk about an action or event that occurred during a specific period of time, you will need to use the structure: "por ___ años" or "por ____ meses", depending on the amount of time that you want to specify. The word "por" is equivalent, in this case, to "for" in the English phrase "for 10 years", "for 4 weeks."

Use the preterite to say when an action or event started or finished.

El espectáculo comenzó a las 10 de la mañana. *(The show started at 10 in the morning.)*

Notice that often the verbs used are directly connected with the meaning of starting or ending:

comenzar *(to begin)*

terminar *(to end)*

empezar *(to start)*

finalizar *(to finish)*

Ser and Estar in the Preterite

These verbs are quite important for my students, as they are very common verbs and you will be using them regularly for almost everything you want to express. First, let's remember quickly the difference between the two:

Ser is used to describe an **essential** characteristic, a feature that is permanent, such as shape, size, color, personality, among others.

Estar is used to describe a temporary state, condition, or location.

Ser and Estar are irregular verbs and they maintain this characteristic in the preterite. For that reason, I ask my students to learn them separately and to help you with this, here is a list of the conjugation for Ser and Estar in the preterite.

Verb: **Ser** (to be)

yo fuí

tu fuiste

él / ella fue

nosotros fuimos

ustedes fueron

ellos fueron

Remember that at the beginning of this lesson, I told you there were two different ways of expressing the past in Spanish, the preterite and the imperfect? This table that I just taught you expresses the verb Ser in the preterite so it means that it will be used to describe a way of being that is completed or definite; in other words, that it has a beginning and an ending. See these examples:

Él fue un buen hombre *(He was a good man (now he is gone))*

Nosotros fuimos amigos *(We were friends (now we are not))*

In the above sentences, the speaker expresses a complete action in the past that is no longer a true statement.

Now let's take a look at another popular verb: **Estar** (to be)

yo estuve

tú estuviste

él / ella estuvo

nosotros estuvimos

ustedes estuvieron

ellos estuvieron

Again, the verb Estar in the above list is in the preterite tense and it expresses a finished action, something that is complete. Let me clarify this idea with some examples:

Ellos estuvieron enamorados *(They were in love)*

Ella estuvo en Europa *(She has been to Europe)*

As you can see, especially in the second example, the action is completed and the state the verb refers to is no longer true.

Time Expressions to use with the Preterite

There are some words and phrases that will help you identify when a sentence is in the preterite and will come in handy when you want to state the time of a past action or event. Some of them may be familiar and I suggest that you read them carefully and study them for 15 minutes.

Ayer *(yesterday)*

Anteayer *(the day before yesterday)*

la semana pasada *(last week)*

el mes pasado *(last month)*

el lunes pasado *(last Monday)*

el año pasado *(last year)*

el otro día *(the other day)*

entonces *(then)*

hace dos meses *(two months ago)*

hace dos años *(two years ago)*

durante tres días *(for three days)*

esta mañana *(this morning)*

esta tarde *(this afternoon)*

Notice that the last two time expressions refer to a time in the day that is already in the past; for example, you can say this morning if you are talking in the afternoon or say this afternoon if you are talking in the evening.

How to form affirmative, negative, and interrogative sentences in the Preterite

The examples I have shared with you so far are all in the affirmative, but it is useful to review the rules here. To make an affirmative sentence in the preterite, you should use the following structure:

Subject + conjugated verb in the preterite + object/rest of the sentence

See the following example:

Ella (subject) escuchó (conjugated verb) un ruido (object/rest of the sentence)

She heard a noise

As I always tell my students, you can hide the subject in the verb because the ending - the conjugation - will determine the subject you are referring to, along with the context:

Escuchó un ruido *(She heard a noise)*

Negative sentences

The negative form in Spanish is usually quite easy to learn because you only need to place the word **no** in the right position. Here is an example:

Ella no escribió la carta *(She did not write the letter)*

The word **no** goes immediately before the verb.

Subject + no + conjugated verb in the preterite + object/rest of the sentence

Eg.: Nosotros no cantamos anoche *(We did not sing last night)*

Sometimes you can find other negative words that express the same idea, and take the place of the word **no**. Take a look at these examples:

Ella **nunca** escribió la carta *(She never wrote the letter)*

Él **jamás** bailó tango *(He never danced to tango music)*

While the meaning is similar, using the words jamás and nunca really emphasizes on the negation.

Interrogative sentences

Take a look at the following variations. What is the difference between them?

¿Ella vivió aquí? (*Did she live here?*)

¿Vivió ella aquí? (*Did she live here?*)

¿Aquí vivió ella? (*Did she live here?*)

My students always ask me why there are so many ways of asking questions in Spanish and I tell them that this is in fact an advantage that they should take, at least with simple sentences. It means they will hardly ever be wrong, even if they find it a little confusing at first.

Yes, there is more than one way of forming questions, just like with the other tenses we discussed before. And it doesn't mean that you can take it lightly and disregard it as something unimportant. In fact, the first and last sentences emphasize on one of the elements that comprise it: he subject (¿**Ella** vivió aquí?) or the place (¿**Aquí** vivió ella?). The second sentence is probably the most neutral in meaning - also the most common option. To put it in other words, in order to make interrogative sentences, you can use one of these structures:

1) conjugated verb in the preterite + subject + object/rest of the sentence

Example:

¿Cocinó María una torta la semana pasada? *(Did María bake a cake last week?)*

2) Subject + conjugated verb in the preterite + object/rest of the sentence

Example:

¿María cocinó una torta la semana pasada? *(Did María bake a cake last week?)*

3) Time expression + conjugated verb in the preterite + object + subject

¿La semana pasada cocinó una torta María? *(Did María bake a cake last week?)*

Remember to add the question marks both at the beginning and ending of the sentence.

When the sentences become more complex, it may be difficult at this early stage to identify which part should go at the beginning of the sentence if you want to ask a question and do it correctly. While the Spanish language is quite flexible when it comes to the structure of questions, you can avoid stepping into thin ice by using the most common structure:

¿ + conjugated verb in the preterite + subject + object/rest of the sentence + ?

¿Estuvieron ellos en Viena? *(Have they been to Viena?)*

Remember that there are a number of verbs in Spanish that are called irregular and they change their ending when conjugated for different subjects, in different tenses. Because this book is intended for beginners, we are not going to cover those verbs for now, but you should take this into account because not all verbs will have the standard conjugations we have revised for regular verbs.

Now that you know all about the preterite, it's time to grab a pencil and practice! Remember to study the lesson for 45 minutes before completing the exercises and write down any questions you may have. Then check again and try to find the answers within the pages of the book.

Exercises

Exercise 1: Turn the following verbs into the preterite, according to each subject.

yo (escuchar) _____

tú (asistir) _____

él (esconder) _____

ella (llegar) _____

nosotros (comprar) _____

ustedes (ganar) _____

ellos (decidir) _____

ellas (gastar) _____

Exercise 2: Which one is correct? Choose the right conjugation of the verbs Ser and Estar in the preterite tense for each subject.

Verb: Ser

Yo fuimos – fui – fue

Tú fui – fueron – fuiste

Ella fue – fui – fuimos

Nosotros fueron – fuimos – fue

Ustedes fuimos – fui – fueron

Él fueron – fuiste - fue

Verb: Estar

Ella estuve – estuvimos - estuvo

Tú estuvimos – estuviste - estuvo

Él estuvieron – estuvo – estuvimos

Nosotros estuvo – estuvieron - estuvimos

Ellos estuve – estuvieron - estuvimos

Ustedes estuvo – estuvieron - estuve

Ellas estuve – estuviste - estuvieron

Exercise 3: Write sentences using the given cue and an appropriate conjugation of the verb in Preterite Tense.

Lucía (gastar) su dinero en zapatos

_____

Paola (escribir) tres cartas la semana pasada

_____

Federico y Luis (visitar) la ciudad hace un mes

_____

Su madre (estar) en Viena hace tres años

_____

At the end of the book, you will find the Unit 13 Key with the correct answers so you can check your progress.

Words You Didn't Know You Knew		
Liberty- libertad	Local- local	Medicine- medicina
Mineral- mineral	Minute- minuto	Model- modelo
Moment- momento	National- nacional	Natural- natural

Grammar Unit 14: Adjectives: Gender and Number

In a previous lesson, I taught you all about nouns and how the Spanish language categorizes them into feminine or masculine. That concept is in many ways related to what I am about to teach you: Gender and Number in Adjectives.

Take a look at these examples:

La mesa es redonda (*The table is round*)

El gato es pequeño (*The cat is small*)

In Spanish, nouns and adjectives have gender and number. You will use adjectives to describe how something is. If the noun it describes is feminine, the adjective will take a feminine form; if the noun is masculine, the adjective will agree with it and present a masculine form.

Most common adjectives end in: -**e**, -**o**, or consonant. To form the feminine form, you must write the ending –**a** instead of the –**o**. There are some interesting rules to follow when you want to describe nouns using an adjective. Let me share them with you:

- Most adjectives ending in –**o** are masculine:

El vino rico; El niño delgado; El hombre Viejo (*the delicious wine; the thin boy, the old man*)

- Most adjectives that end in –**a** are feminine:

La flor bella; La mujer alta; La casa pequeña (*the beautiful flower; the tall woman; the small house*)

- Adjectives that end in –**e** do not change their ending according to gender. However, they change to agree with a singular or plural noun (*we'll go back to this in a minute*).

La casa grande; El plato grande; La mujer valiente; El hombre valiente (*the big house; the large plate; the brave woman; the brave man*)

- Adjectives that end in –ista also do not change their endings according to gender. They remain in the same form:

El hombre egoísta; la mujer egoísta *(the selfish man; the selfish woman)*

- Most adjectives that end in a consonant do not change for feminine or masculine nouns, but they do change to agree in number.

La mano veloz; el coche veloz; la mujer joven; el hombre joven *(the fast hand; the fast car; the young woman; the young man)*

- The general form of adjectives end in –o. Then you can make the necessary changes to make them agree with the subject they modify; for example, adding–**a** for feminine nouns, or –**s** for plural nouns.

- Adjectives that end in –**or**, -**án**, -**ín** or –**ón** change to agree with feminine nouns by adding–**a** at the ending:

Hombre fumador *(smoker (man))*

Mujer fumadora *(smoker (woman))*

Niño encantador *(charming boy)*

Niña encantadora *(charming girl)*

Gato juguetón *(playful cat (male))*

Gata juguetona *(playful cat (female))*

Notice that the ending –**ón** changes to –**ona** to form the feminine and the written accent mark is left out.

- One exception are the adjectives ending in –**erior**, which do not change to form the feminine

La mesa superior; el piso superior *(The upper table; the upper floor)*

Let's Talk About the Plural

In Spanish, you will need the letter –s to form the plural; however there are a few exceptions, where –es is needed. Here are some examples:

El cuaderno Amarillo (*The yellow notebook*)

Los cuadernos amarillos (*The yellow notebooks*)

Notice that in Spanish, not only the noun takes–s at the ending to form the plural, but also the adjective that describes it takes–s.

When the adjective ends in a vowel, you will simply need to add–s to the ending:

Bueno / buenos

Alto / altos

Fuerte / fuertes

Inteligente / inteligentes

Lindo / lindos

Grande / grandes

Nuevo / nuevos

Rico / ricos

However, when an adjective ends in a consonant, you will need to add –es to the ending to form the plural. Here are some examples:

Joven / jóvenes

Débil / débiles

Fácil / fáciles

One special note about adjectives that end in a consonant: when the consonant is Z, they change –z for –c and then add –es:

Feliz / felices

So, in this lesson I have taught you the basics about adjectives in Spanish so you can start using them in conversation and feel comfortable doing so. Adjectives, in general, follow the noun, although their position within a sentence may change for poetic reasons or for emphasis.

Remember that most common adjectives take 4 forms:

Masculine singular: lindo (pretty)

Masculine plural: lindos

Feminine singular: linda

Feminine plural: lindas

Now it's time for a little practice! Before you complete the exercises, study the lesson for 20 minutes, paying special attention to the rules for using adjectives.

Exercises

Exercise 1: Match the adjectives with the nouns. Use your knowledge of the verb "to be" in Spanish.

María y Amalia – jóven

Mi madre – inteligente

El perro – grande

Las flores – hermoso

El auto – nuevo

Su amiga – pobre

Lucía, Ana y Susana – honesto

Los pájaros - loco

Exercise 2: Write the feminine and plural forms of the following verbs. Indicate when a verb stays the same for the feminine.

fumador _____

juguetón _____

ladrón _____

veloz _____

inteligente _____

grande _____

lindo _____

infantil _____

popular _____

rico_____

At the end of the book, you will find the Unit 14 Key with the correct answers so you can check your progress.

Words You Didn't Know You Knew		
Normal normal	Number número	Object objeto
Ocean océano	Office oficina	Paper papel
Police policía	Public público	Radio radio
Romantic romántico	Solution solución	Terminal terminal
Traditional tradicional	Urban urbano	University universidad

Pronunciation Unit 15

While you will definitely need to actually listen to people speak Spanish to understand and repeat the sounds, this lesson on the vowels and the complete alphabet will be of help when it comes to making your first immersion in the language.

A mistake most of my students make is to be too shy about speaking in Spanish. They are afraid to sound weird and in trying to avoid this, they end up sounding strange both in English and in Spanish. Learning a language is like riding a boat down a river. If you are in the English boat, it will not be enough to put only one leg onboard the Spanish boat; it is unsafe and you could fall into the current. You have to make a choice: I f you want to speak Spanish as natives do, you have to jump into the new boat and let the river guide you; forget about the English sounds and have fun learning a new array of sounds that make up this wonderful language and culture.

The Spanish Vowels

The vowels have a clear, crisp sound. There are strong and weak vowels, depending on the movement the mouth makes when pronouncing them. A, E and O are strong vowels, and I, U are weak vowels. We can say that the vowels in Spanish have only one sound. Here they are:

a – A (as in **A**pple)

e – E (as in **E**lephant)

i – e (and in **e**conomy)

o – Oh (as in **oi**l)

u – U (as in G**oo**gle)

Remember that in conversation, people tend to join these vowels together, especially when there is a diphthong and although it may sound confusing, you will master them with practice.

The Alphabet

According to the latest edition of the Dictionary of the Real Academia Española, the highest authority that regulates the Spanish language, there is only one letter in the Spanish Alphabet that does not exist in the English Alphabet and it expresses a special sound that is a characteristic of the language. We are talking about the letter Ñ and it sounds like the first two in Gnome.

There used to be other letters or combinations of existing letters that were part of the alphabet, such as Ll, Rr, and Ch, but they were recently eliminated as separate letters and they are now considered a repetition or association of letters instead.

This is our current alphabet, called in Spanish abecedario:

a (a)

b (be)

c (ce)

d (de)

e (e)

f (efe)

g (ge)

h (ache)

i (i)

j (jota)

k (ka)

l (ele)

m (eme)

n (ene)

ñ (eñe)

o (o)

p (pe)

q (ku)

r (ere)

s (ese)

t (te)

u (u)

v (ve)

w (doble ve /uve doble)

x (equis)

y (i griega)

z (zeta)

Vocabulary

Regular verbs in Spanish

In this list, I have included some of the most common regular verbs in Spanish, their pronunciation, and English equivalent.

Abandonar /a-ban-doh-´nar *(To quit)*

Abrir /a-´brir *(To open)*

Absorber /ab-sor-´ber *(To absorb)*

Abusar /a-bu-´sar *(To abuse)*

Acabar /a-ka-´bar *(To finish)*

Acampar /a-kam-´par *(To camp)*

Acelerar /a-ce-le-´rar *(To accelerate)*

Aceptar /a-cep-´tar *(To accept)*

Admitir /ad-mi-´tir *(To admit)*

Adorar /a-do-´rar *(To adore)*

Alquilar /al-ki-´lar *(To rent)*

Amar /a-´mar *(To love)*

Andar /an-´dar *(To walk)*

Aprehender /a-pre-en-´der *(To apprehend)*

Aprender /a-pren-´der *(To learn)*

Asistir /a-sis-´tir/ *(To attend)*

Ayudar /a-yu-´dar *(To help)*

Bailar /bai-´lar *(To dance)*

Bañar /ba-´niar *(To shower)*

Barrer /ba-´rrer *(To sweep)*

Beber /be-´ber *(To drink)*

Besar /be-´sar *(To kiss)*

Buscar /bus-´kar *(To look for)*

Caminar /ka-mi-´nar *(To walk)*

Cantar /kan-´tar *(To sing)*

Cocinar /ko-ci-´nar *(To cook)*

Comer /ko-´mer *(To eat)*

Comprar /kom-´prar *(To buy)*

Comprender /kom-prend-´der *(To understand)*

Conceder /kon-ce-´der *(To concede)*

Contestar /kon-tes-´tar *(To answer)*

Correr /ko-´rrer *(To run)*

Cortar /kor-´tar *(To cut)*

Creer /kre-ér *(To believe)*

Cubrir /ku-´brir *(To cover)*

Deber /de-´ber *(To owe)*

Decidir /de-ci-´dir *(To decide)*

Dejar /de-´jar *(To allow)*

Depender /de-pen-´der *(To depend)*

Desayunar /de-sa-yu-´nar *(To have breakfast)*

Describir /des-kri-´bir *(To describe)*

Desear /de-se-ár *(To wish)*

Discutir /dis-ku-´tir *(To argue)*

Enamorarse /e-na-mo-´rar-se *(To fall in love)*

Enseñar /en-se-niár *(To teach)*

Entrar (en) /en-´trar (en) *(To enter)*

Enviar /en-vi-ár *(To send)*

Esconder /es-kon-´der *(To hide)*

Escribir /es-kri-´bir *(To write)*

Escuchar /es-ku-´char *(To listen)*

Esperar /es-pe-´rar *(To wait)*

Estudiar /es-tu-´diar *(To study, to revise)*

Exceder /ec-ce-´der *(To exceed)*

Existir /ec-cis-´tir *(To exist)*

Firmar /fir-´mar *(To sign)*

Ganar /ga-´nar *(To win)*

Gastar /gas-´tar *(To spend)*

Hablar /a-´blar *(To talk)*

Lavar /la-´var *(To wash)*

Leer /le-ér *(To read)*

Llegar /lle-´gar *(To arrive)*

Llevar /lle-´var *(To carry)*

Mandar /man-´dar *(To order)*

Meter /me-´ter *(To put into)*

Mirar /mi-´rar *(To look)*

Nadar /na-ˈdar *(To swim)*

Necesitar /ne-ce-si-ˈtar *(To need)*

Olvidar /ol-vi-ˈdar *(To forget)*

Omitir /o-mi-ˈtir *(To omit)*

Partir /par-ˈtir *(To leave)*

Permitir /per-mi-ˈtir *(To allow)*

Poseer /po-se-ér *(To possess)*

Practicar /prac-ti-ˈkar *(To practice)*

Preguntar /pre-gun-ˈtar *(To ask)*

Prender /pren-ˈder *(To switch on)*

Preparar /pre-pa-ˈrar *(To prepare)*

Proceder /pro-ce-ˈder *(To proceed)*

Prometer /pro-me-ˈter *(To promise)*

Regresar /re-gre-ˈsar *(To return)*

Reparar /re-pa-ˈrar *(To repair)*

Romper /rom-ˈper *(To break)*

Saludar /sa-lu-ˈdar *(To greet)*

Sorprender /sor-pren-ˈder *(To surprise)*

Subir /su-ˈbir *(To go up)*

Sufrir /su-ˈfrir *(To suffer)*

Tejer /te-ˈjer *(To knit)*

Temer /te-ˈmer *(To fear)*

Tocar /to-ˈkar *(To touch)*

Toser /to-´ser *(To cough)*

Trabajar /tra-ba-´jar *(To work)*

Unir /u-´nir *(To unite)*

Usar /u-´sar *(To use)*

Vender /ven-´der *(To sell)*

Viajar /via-´jar *(To travel)*

Visitar /vi-si-´tar *(To visit)*

Votar /vo-´tar *(To vote)*

Numbers

In this lesson, I will teach you the numbers one by one. Numbers in written form can be found in official or administrative documents or where you wish to clarify an amount expressed in numbers, such as prices, quantity, etc.

I have highlighted some parts of the written numbers that will help you figure out the rules for writing them down flawlessly. Take a look and then continue reading for further explanation:

0 – cero

1 – uno

2 – dos

3 – tres

4 – cuatro

5 – cinco

6 – seis

7 –siete

8 – ocho

9 – nueve

10 – **diez**

11 – once

12 – doce

13 – trece

14 – catorce

15 – quince

16 – **diec**iséis

17 – **diec**isiete

18 – **diec**iocho

19 – **diec**inueve

20 – **veinte**

21 – **veint**iuno

22 – **veinti**dós

23 – **veinti**trés

24 – **veinti**cuatro

25 – **veinti**cinco

26 – **veinti**séis

27 – **veinti**siete

28 – **veinti**ocho

29 – **veinti**nueve

30 – **treinta**

31 – treinta **y uno**

32 – treinta **y dos**

33 – treinta **y tres**

34 – treinta **y cuatro**

35 – treinta **y cinco**

36 – treinta **y seis**

37 – treinta **y siete**

38 – treinta **y ocho**

39 – treinta **y nueve**

40 - cuar**enta**

41 – cuarenta y uno

42 – cuarenta y dos

43 – cuarenta y tres

44 – cuarenta y cuatro

45 – cuarenta y cinco

46 – cuarenta y seis

47 – cuarenta y siete

48 – cuarenta y ocho

49 – cuarenta y nueve

50 – cincu**enta**

51 – cincuenta y uno

52 – cincuenta y dos

53 – cincuenta y tres

54 – cincuenta y cuatro

55 – cincuenta y cinco

56 – cincuenta y seis

57 – cincuenta y siete

58 – cincuenta y ocho

59 – cincuenta y nueve

60 – ses**enta**

61 – sesenta y uno

62 – sesenta y dos

63 – sesenta y tres

64 – sesenta y cuatro

65 – sesenta y cinco

66 – sesenta y seis

67 – sesenta y siete

68 – sesenta y ocho

69 – sesenta y nueve

70 – set**enta**

71 – setenta y uno

72 – setenta y dos

73 – setenta y tres

74 – setenta y cuatro

75 – setenta y cinco

76 – setenta y seis

77 – setenta y siete

78 – setenta y ocho

79 – setenta y nueve

80 - och**enta**

81 – ochenta y uno

82 – ochenta y dos

83 – ochenta y tres

84 – ochenta y cuatro

85 – ochenta y cinco

86 – ochenta y seis

87 – ochenta y siete

88 – ochenta y ocho

89 – ochenta y nueve

90 – nov**enta**

91 – noventa y uno

92 – noventa y dos

93 – noventa y tres

94 – noventa y cuatro

95 – noventa y cinco

96 – noventa y seis

97 – noventa y siete

98 – noventa y ocho

99 – noventa y nueve

100 – **cien**

Learning numbers **uno** to **nueve** is key because it will be so much easier for you to remember the rest of the numbers, no matter what figure you want to express.

Numbers from cero to veintinueve are written as one word, also tens and hundreds are written as one word: *treinta, cincuenta, ochenta, cien, doscientos and so on.*

Numbers from treinta y uno on are written as two words with the use of the conjunction y (and): *treinta y tres, sesenta y nueve, ochenta y siete.*

Except for *diez (ten), veinte (twenty) and treinta (thirty),* all tens have *–enta* endings.

My students usually ask, why should we learn numbers? My answer is because you want to be able to read out loud a particular year, your age, your address, your phone number, the hotel room you are staying in, or to get a price right. Numbers are part of our everyday life and quite often you will hear them in speech, ending up lost in the conversation if you do not know them properly. So my advice for this lesson is: study the structure behind the list (hint: I highlighted the most important cues there for you) and go through any newspaper, magazine, or even tune into CNBC channel and whenever you see a figure, try to think of the written number in Spanish. If this is hard to do, you can grab a pen and the newspaper we talked about and write down the written word next to any number. Do this for 15 minutes and allow your brain to take the time it needs to recall the figure. You will notice that with practice, you will be able to tell the numbers in Spanish. And please do start by saying and writing down your age, phone number, and any other personal identification number you have.

We will get on with numbers above **cien** in another lesson to come.

A note about numbers:

You can use numbers to talk about the quantity of things and people.

Take a look at these examples:

Una rosa *(one rose)*

Veinte sillas *(twenty chairs)*

Dos personas *(two people)*

Un oso *(one bear)*

In the case of un/una, the use depends on the "gender of the noun." The rule is:

Un – for counting "masculine" nouns

Una – for counting "feminine" nouns

Exercises

Do not forget to practice! You can start with the following exercises.

Exercise 1: Write the correct number.

a. 16 _____

b. 6 _____

c. 23 _____

d. 9 _____

e. 89 _____

f. 29 _____

g. 54 _____

h. 75 _____

i. 13 _____

j. 92 _____

k. 21 _____

l. 1 _____

m. 47 _____

At the end of the book, you will find the Unit 15 Key with the correct answers so you can check your progress.

Colors

What would life be without colors? You can use the following words to express anything related to colors

Amarillo (*Yellow)*

Anaranjado (*Orange)*

Azul *(Blue)*

Blanco (*White)*

Celeste (*Light Blue*)

Gris (*Grey)*

Marrón (*Brown)*

Negro (*Black)*

Rojo (*Red)*

Rosa (*Pink)*

Violeta (*Violet)*

Verde (*Green)*

Jobs and Occupations

I will now teach you a list of words to describe jobs and occupations. This will come in handy when you want to say what you do for a living!

Abogado (*Lawyer*)

Ama de Casa (*Housewife*)

Artista (*Artist*)

Arquitecto (*Architect*)

Biólogo (*Biologist*)

Bombero (*Firefighter*)

Cajero (*Cashier*)

Carpintero (*Carpenter*)

Chofer (*Driver*)

Contador (*Accountant*)

Doctor (*Doctor*)

Estudiante (*Student*)

Fotógrafo (*Photographer*)

Ingeniero (*Engineer*)

Panadero (*Baker*)

Peluquero (*Hairdresser*)

Piloto (*Pilot*)

Pintor (*Painter*)

Policía (*Police man/woman*)

Presidente (*President*)

Profesor (*Professor)*

Psicólogo (*Psychologist)*

Redactor (*Writer)*

Secretaria (*Secretary)*

Countries

This vocabulary lesson will come in handy when you are abroad or talking with people from other countries. Take a look at this short list of countries and nationalities:

África /ˈa-fri-ka *(Africa)*

Alemania /a-le-ˈma-nia *(Germany)*

Argentina /ar-jen-ˈti-na *(Argentina)*

Brasil /bra-ˈsil *(Brazil)*

Canadá /ka-na-ˈda *(Canada)*

Chile /ˈchi-le *(Chile)*

China /ˈchi-na *(China)*

Colombia /ko-ˈlom-bia *(Colombia)*

Egipto /e-ˈjip-to *(Egypt)*

España /es-ˈpa-nia *(Spain)*

Estados Unidos /es-ˈta-dos u-ˈni-dos *(The US)*

Francia /ˈfran-cia *(France)*

Inglaterra /in-gla-ˈte-rra *(England)*

Italia /i-ˈta-lia *(Italy)*

Japón /ja-ˈpon *(Japan)*

México /ˈme-ji-co *(Mexico)*

Portugal /por-tu-ˈgal *(Portugal)*

Rusia /ˈrru-sia *(Russia)*

Suiza /ˈsui-za *(Switzerland)*

Nationalities

Notice that nationalities do not take capital letter at the beginning.

África: africano / africana

Alemania: alemán / alemana

Argentina: argentino / argentina

Brasil: brasileño / brasileña

Canadá: canadiense

Chile: chileno / chilena

China: chino / china

Colombia: colombiano / colombiana

Estados Unidos: estadounidense

Egipto: egipcio / egipcia

España: español / española

Francia: francés / francesa

Inglaterra: inglés / inglesa

Italia: italiano / italiana

Japón: japonés / japonesa

México: mexicano / mexicana

Portugal: portugués / portuguesa

Rusia: ruso / rusa

Suiza: suizo / suiza

Items in the Kitchen

This is a vocabulary lesson that my students love because whether you are a guy or a girl, you certainly will use these words when you need to ask for something in the kitchen. In this lesson, you will find not only separate words that name objects, but also phrases that may be used in the context of a kitchen. My suggestion for this unit is that you randomly pick a few objects and start naming them in Spanish when you need to call for them in your house. For example, instead of saying "I'm putting away the dishes," you can change it to "I'm putting away the platos." That way you will be incorporating the vocabulary into your everyday life and it will become easier, faster.

Let's start with the larger objects and appliances

La bacha /la ´ba-cha (*The sink*)

El fregadero /el fre-ga-´de-ro (*The sink*)

La heladera /la e-la-´de-ra (*The refrigerator*)

El refrigerador /el re-fri-je-ra-´dor (*The refrigerator*)

La cocina /la ko-´ci-na (*The stove*)

La mesada /la me-´sa-da (*The countertop*)

La cafetera /la ka-fe-´te-ra (*The coffee maker*)

El microondas /el mi-kro-ón-das (*The microwave*)

La tostadora /la tos-ta-´do-ra (*The toaster*)

La batidora /la ba-ti-´do-ra (*The mixer*)

El horno /el ´or-no (*The oven*)

La licuadora /la li-kua-´do-ra (*The blender*)

What do you need in order to set the table? Here are some words you will enjoy:

El mantel /el man-´tel (*The tablecloth*)

Los platos /los ´pla-tos (*The plates*)

El vaso /el ´va-so (*The glass*)

La copa /la ´ko-pa (*The cup*)

El cuchillo /ku-´chi-yo (*The knife*)

La cuchara /la ku-´cha-ra (*The spoon*)

El tenedor /el te-ne-´dor (*The fork*)

La servilleta /la ser-vi-´ye-ta (*The napkin*)

Now you are ready to set the table. But what if you need to prepare your food? These are the words you will want to use:

La sartén /la sar-´ten (*The frying pan*)

La olla /la ´o-ya (*The saucepan*)

La cacerola /la ka-ce-´ro-la (*The casserole dish*)

El destapador /el des-ta-pa-´dor (*The bottle opener*)

El rallador /el rra-ya-´dor (*The grater*)

La plancha /la ´plan-cha (*The iron*)

La tetera /la te-´te-ra (*The teapot*)

La tapa /la ´ta-pa (*The lid*)

Now, I will teach you some of the phrases that are commonly used in Spanish for activities around the kitchen.

Poner la mesa /po-´ner la ´me-sa (*To set the table*)

Preparar la cena /pre-pa-´rar la ´ce-na (*To prepare dinner*)

Lavar los platos /la-´var los ´pla-tos (*To do the dishes*)

Hornear una torta /or-´near u-na ´tor-ta (*To bake a cake*)

Pelar las cebollas /pe-´lar las ce-´bo-yas (*To peel the onions*)

Barrer el piso /ba-´rrer el ´pi-so (*To sweep the floor*)

Lavar los vegetales /la-´var los ve-ge-´ta-les (*To wash the vegetables*)

Cocer las verduras /ko-´cer las ver-´du-ras (*To cook the vegetables*)

Hervir los huevos /er-´vir los ´ue-vos (*To boil the eggs*)

Hervir el agua /er-´vir el ´a-gua (To boil water)

Encender el horno /en-cen-´der el ´or-no *(To turn on the oven)*

Cortar en rebanadas /kor-´tar en re-ba-´na-das (*To chop*)

Cortar en porciones /kor-´tar en por-´cio-nes (*To cut into slices*)

Picar /pi-´kar (*To grind*)

Precalentar el horno /pre-ka-len-´tar el ´or-no (*To preheat the oven*)

Items in the Office

In this vocabulary lesson, I will teach you a number of words to use around your office. This will be quite easy for you to learn because you can immediately start calling the names of the items around you in your office. Let's begin!

La oficina / la o-fi-´ci-na (*The office*)

El escritorio / el es-kri-´to-rio (*The desk*)

La computadora / la kom-pu-ta-´do-ra (*The computer*)

La silla / la ´si-lla (*The chair*)

La impresora / la im-pre-´so-ra (*The printer*)

La pluma / la ´plu-ma (*The pen*)

La lapicera / la la-pi-´ce-ra (*The pen*)

El lápiz / el ´la-piz (*The pencil*)

El marcador / el mar-ka-´dor (*The marker*)

El cuaderno / el kua-´der-no (*The notebook*)

Las hojas / las ´o-jas (*The sheets*)

La grapadora / la gra-pa-´do-ra (*The stapler*)

El fax / el facs (*The fax machine*)

La calculadora / la kal-ku-la-´do-ra (*The calculator*)

El fichero / el fi-´che-ro (*The cabinet*)

La carpeta / la kar-´pe-ta (*The folder*)

Key

Key: Unit 1 Subject Pronouns

Exercise 1

a. ellas

b. nosotros

c. él

e. ellos

f. nosotros

g. ellos

h. nosotras

Exercise 2

a. ella

b. él

c. ellos

d. él

e. nosotros

f. ella

g. ella

h. él

i. él

j. ellas

Key: Unit 2: Gender of Nouns

Exercise 1

a. dieciséis

b. seis

c. veintitrés

d. nueve

e. ochenta y nueve

f. veintinueve

g. cincuenta y cuatro

h. setenta y cinco

i. trece

j. noventa y dos

k. veintiuno

l. uno

m. cuarenta y siete

Key: Unit 3: Plural Nouns

Exercise 1

a. la bota – female

b. el mensaje – male

c. el maestro – male

d. el cliente / la cliente – male and female

e. el gato – male

f. la fiesta – female

g. el automóvil – male

h. el estudiante / la estudiante – male and female

i. el asistente / la asistente – male and female

j. la ropa – female

k. la costumbre – female

l. la decisión – female

m. la felicidad – female

n. el tema – male

Exercise 2

a. el

b. el

c. el

d. la

e. la

f. la

g. la

h. la

i. la

j. el/la

Key: Unit 4: Definite and Indefinite Articles

Exercise 1

a. plural

b. singular

c. plural

d. plural

e. plural

f. singular

g. singular

h. plural

i. singular

j. singular

Exercise 2

a. vasos

b. letras

c. personas

d. bolsos

e. juegos

f. profesoras

g. pasiones

h. caminos

i. viajes

j. matices

k. chocolates

l. mansiones

m. sabores

n. dulces

o. sillones

p. actrices

q. mapas

r. amigos

s. ratones

t. uvas

u. salones

v. barcos

w. manzanas

x. aviones

Key: Unit 5: Verb Haber in Spanish

Exercise 1

a. el

b. los

c. la

d. las

e. los

f. la

g. el

h. la

i. los

j. el

k. las

l. los

m. el

n. los

Exercise 2

a. definite

b. indefinite

c. definite

d. indefinite

e. definite

f. indefinite

g. definite

h. indefinite

Exercise 3

a. El libro

b. El profesor

c. Unos gatos

d. Unas flores

e. La bandera

f. La casa

g. Un televisor

h. La cama

i. Unas galletitas

Key: Unit 6: Regular Verbs in Spanish

Exercise 1

a. Hay una TV / no hay una TV

b. Hay un perfume / no hay un perfume

c. Hay un gato / no hay un gato

d. Hay una planta / no hay una planta

e. Hay una heladera / no hay una heladera

f. Hay un sillón / no hay un sillón

g. Hay un plato / no hay un plato

h. Hay un teléfono / no hay un teléfono

i. Hay una estantería / no hay una estantería

j. Hay unas sillas / no hay unas sillas

Exercise 2

a. Hay dos gatos en el techo

b. Hay un niño en el jardín

c. Hay dos personas en la calle

d. Hay cinco sillas en la sala

e. Hay tres escuelas en el barrio

f. Hay un libro sobre la mesa

g. Hay una computadora en el escritorio

h. Hay dos TVs en la casa

i. Hay un peine en mi cartera

j. Hay un cuadro en la pared

Key: Unit 7: The Present Tense

Exercise 1

Abrir

Aprender

Andar

Esperar

Recibir

Partir

Vender

Vivir

Pagar

Desear

Estudiar

Buscar

Caminar

Hablar

Dejar

Trabajar

Exercise 2

Él asiste

Yo escribo

Nosotras lavamos

Ella sufre

Ustedes practican

Tú comes

Él alquila

Nosotros discutimos

Ellos preguntan

Ellas compran

Tú bailas

Yo gano

Exercise 3

Yo firmo

Tú firmas

Él / ella firma

Nosotros firmamos

Ustedes firman

Ellos /ellas firman

Yo estudio

Tú estudias

Él / ella estudia

Nosotros estudiamos

Ustedes estudian

Ellos /ellas estudian

Yo enseño

Tú enseñas

Él / ella enseña

Nosotros enseñamos

Ustedes enseñan

Ellos /ellas enseñan

Yo gano

Tú ganas

Él / ella gana

Nosotros ganamos

Ustedes ganan

Ellos / ellas ganan

Yo busco

Tú buscas

Él / ella busca

Nosotros buscamos

Ustedes buscan

Ellos / ellas buscan

Yo gasto

Tú gastas

Él / ella gasta

Nosotros gastamos

Ustedes gastan

Ellos / ellas gastan

Yo subo

Tú subes

Él / ella sube

Nosotros subimos

Ustedes suben

Ellos / ellas suben

Yo temo

Tú temes

Él / ella teme

Nosotros tememos

Ustedes temen

Ellos / ellas temen

Yo camino

Tú caminas

Él / ella camina

Nosotros caminamos

Ustedes caminan

Ellos / ellas caminan

Yo cocino

Tú cocinas

Él / ella cocina

Nosotros cocinamos

Ustedes cocinan

Ellos / ellas cocinan

Yo entro

Tú entras

Él / ella entra

Nosotros entramos

Ustedes entran

Ellos / ellas entran

Yo pregunto

Tú preguntas

Él / ella pregunta

Nosotros preguntamos

Ustedes preguntan

Ellos / ellas preguntan

Yo discuto

Tú discutes

Él / ella discute

Nosotros discutimos

Ustedes discuten

Ellos / ellas discuten

Yo bebo

Tú bebes

Él / ella bebe

Nosotros bebemos

Ustedes beben

Ellos / ellas beben

Yo como

Tú comes

Él / ella come

Nosotros comemos

Ustedes comen

Ellos / ellas comen

Yo olvido

Tú olvidas

Él / ella olvida

Nosotros olvidamos

Ustedes olvidan

Ellos / ellas olvidan

Yo dejo

Tú dejas

Él / ella deja

Nosotros dejamos

Ustedes dejan

Ellos / ellas dejan

Yo viajo

Tú viajas

Él / ella viaja

Nosotros viajamos

Ustedes viajan

Ellos / ellas viajan

Exercise 4

Hacéis

Habláis

Llegáis

Compráis

Subís

Leéis

Recibís

Entráis

Buscáis

Estudiáis

Pagáis

Amáis

Camináis

Describís

Key: Unit 8: Present Progressive in Spanish

Exercise 1

Ella sabe

Nosotros abrimos

Él come

Ellos contestan

Usted baila

Tú aprendes

Yo regreso

Ustedes ganan

Él sorprende

Ellos saludan

Usted trabaja

Ella teme

Nosotros viajamos

Tú olvidas

Yo nado

Ustedes miran

Exercise 2

nosotros usamos

él/ella/usted tose

ustedes/ellos/ellas llegan

yo necesito

él/ella/usted toca

tú miras

ustedes/ellos/ellas compran

él come

nosotros acampamos

ustedes/ellos/ellas admiten

tú comprendes

yo acelero

él/ella/usted canta

tú dejas

nosotros desayunamos

ustedes/ellos/ellas barren

él/ella/usted ayuda

tú describes

él/ella/usted habla

ustedes/ellos/ellas discuten

tú envías

nosotros escuchamos

él/ella/usted prepara

ustedes/ellos/ellas rompen

Key: Unit 9: Ser and Estar, the Verb "To Be" in Spanish

Exercise 1

a. estás

b. está

c. estoy

d. están

e. estamos

f. está

g. están

h. están

i. están

j. están

Exercise 2

a. nosotros

b. tú

c. él/ella/usted

d. yo

e. ustedes/ellos/ellas

Exercise 3

a. yo estoy estudiando

b. ella está cocinando

c. tú estás viajando

d. él está escribiendo

e. nosotros estamos oyendo

f. ellos están cantando

g. ellas están hablando

h. ustedes están bebiendo

i. tú estás mirando

j. nosotras estamos viviendo

k. yo estoy creyendo

l. él está creciendo

m. ella está entrando

n. tú estás subiendo

o. él está sufriendo

p. nosotros estamos trabajando

q. ellos están llegando

r. ellas están diseñando

s. ustedes están caminando

t. tú estás andando

u. nosotras estamos enseñando

v. yo estoy ganando

w. él está leyendo

Exercise 4

a. Ella no está estudiando

b. Nosotros no estamos cocinando

c. Ustedes no están escribiendo

d. Él no está cantando

e. Ellos no están protestando

f. Tú no estás hablando

g. Nosotros no estamos vendiendo

h. Ella no está nadando

i. Tú no estás buscando

j. Ellos no están oyendo

Exercise 5

Ellas no están hablando

¿Están ellas hablando?

Yo no estoy regresando

¿Estoy yo regresando?

Tú no estás sufriendo

¿Estás tú sufriendo?

Nosotros no estamos comiendo

¿Estamos nosotros comiendo?

Él no está ganando

¿Está él ganando?

Ellos no están cantando

¿Están ellos cantando?

No estás caminando

¿Estás caminando?

No estoy estudiando

¿Estoy estudiando?

No estamos practicando

¿Estamos practicando?

Exercise 6

Ella no está cocinando

Tú no estás saliendo

¿Estamos nosotros comiendo?

Ellos están aprendiendo

Key: Unit 10: Possessive Adjectives

Exercise 1

Estoy aburrida - condition

Ella es inteligente - essence

Somos hermanos - essence

Estamos cansados - condition

Ellos están arriba - condition

Es muy bella - essence

La fiesta es en su casa - condition

Está nublado - condition

Es moderna - essence

Está enferma – condition

Exercise 2

La niña no es tímida

¿Es tímida la niña?

No estamos en la oficina

¿Estamos en la oficina?

Ella no es alta

¿Es ella alta?

Él no es médico

¿Es él medico?

Ellos no están hambrientos

¿Están ellos hambrientos?

No está nublado

¿Está nublado?

El niño no está aquí

¿Está el niño aquí?

Yo no soy la hija de Laura

¿Soy yo la hija de Laura?

El pastel no es delicioso

¿Es delicioso el pastel?

La habitación no está desordenada

¿Está la habitación desordenada?

Exercise 3

Soleado - estar

Católico - ser

Aburrido – estar/ser

Contento - estar

Hablando - estar

Carpintero - ser

Doctora - ser

Tu padre - ser

En chile - estar

Moderno - ser

Nuevo - ser

Desordenado – ser/estar

Deprimido - estar

Las 3.15am - ser

De madera - ser

Italiano - ser

Exercise 4

La flor es rosa

El cuadro es moderno

Son las 4.10pm

Estamos deprimidos

Estamos en Argentina

Ellos son profesores

El niño está en la habitación

La mesa es cuadrada

Ella es mi madre

No estamos cansados

Key: Unit 11: The Future Simple Tense

Exercise 1

Tú – tu

Yo – mi

Ella – su

Nosotros – nuestro

Ellos – su

Ustedes – su

Usted – su

Él – su

Exercise 2

mis libros

tu casa

su novia

sus padres

nuestras llaves

su teléfono

sus documentos

Key: Unit 12: More about the Future Tense

Exercise 1

Yo asistiré

Ustedes esperarán

Ellos alquilarán

Ella entrará

Tú buscarás

Él beberá

Nosotros prepararemos

Yo enseñaré

Ustedes preguntarán

Ellos firmarán

Ella caminará

Tú comerás

Él olvidará

Nosotros tomaremos

Yo leeré

Ustedes mandarán

Ellos bailarán

Nosotros ganaremos

Yo escribiré

Ustedes creerán

Ella tocará

Tú viajarás

Él comprenderá

Ella regresará

Tú subirás

Él cocinará

Nosotros llegaremos

Yo venderé

Tú cubrirás

Ellos sonreirán

Exercise 2

Ella no llegará mañana

¿Llegará ella mañana?

Nosotros no seremos abuelos

¿Seremos nosotros abuelos?

Él no vivirá aquí

¿Vivirá él aquí?

Ella no viajará el sábado

¿Viajará ella el sábado?

Tú no visitarás la ciudad

¿Visitarás tú la ciudad?

Ellos no estarán contentos

¿Estarán ellos contentos?

Ustedes no jugarán mañana

¿Jugarán ustedes mañana?

Ella no comprará comida

¿Comprará ella comida?

Exercise 3

Sam y Vane estarán en la ciudad la próxima semana

Ellos visitarán el museo

Vane comprará en las tiendas

Sam caminará por el pueblo

Ellos bailarán en una disco

Ellos no mirarán una película

Sam y Vane alquilarán un auto

Key: Unit 13: The Past Simple Tense: Preterite

Exercise 1

Lucía llega mañana

El atleta corre esta noche

Yo viajo la próxima semana

La artista canta el próximo lunes

Nosotros viajamos el domingo

Su novio regresa en tres días

Yo cocino la cena esta noche

El actor firma autógrafos mañana

Los novios viajan el próximo mes

La tienda abre el martes

El tren sale en tres horas

Exercise 2

Laura va a acampar en el bosque

María va a cocinar la cena

El doctor va a escribir una nota

Nosotros vamos a viajar a Londres

Ellos van a ganar la final

Tú vas a comprar un presente

Juan y Pedro van a aprender francés

Yo voy a pagar la cuenta

La profesora va a preparar la lección

El niño va a romper el vaso

Los hombres van a trabajar

Mi abuela va a cocinar una torta

Key: Unit 14: Adjectives: Gender and Number

Exercise 1

Yo escuché

Tú asististe

Él escondió

Ellos decidieron

Ella llegó

Nosotros compramos

Ustedes ganaron

Ellas gastaron

Exercise 2

yo fui

tú fuiste

ella fue

nosotros fuimos

ustedes fueron

él fue

ella estuvo

tú estuviste

él estuvo

nosotros estuvimos

ellos estuvieron

ustedes estuvieron

ellas estuvieron

Exercise 3

Lucía gastó su dinero en zapatos

Paola escribió tres cartas la semana pasada

Federico y Luis visitaron la ciudad hace un mes

Su madre estuvo en Viena hace tres años

Key: Unit 15: Pronunciation

Exercise 1

María y Amalia son jóvenes

Mi madre es inteligente

El perro es grande

Las flores son hermosas

El auto es nuevo

Su amiga es pobre

Lucía, Ana y Susana son honestas

Los pájaros son locos

Exercise 2

fumador – fumadora – fumadores – fumadoras

juguetón – juguetona – juguetones – juguetonas

ladrón – ladrona – ladrones – ladronas

veloz – veloces

inteligente – inteligentes

grande – grandes

lindo – linda – lindos – lindas

infantil – infantiles

popular – populares

rico – rica – ricos – ricas

Are you Interested in Learning More Spanish

If so, there are many great e-books on the Amazon Marketplace that can help. Two of the books that we recommend are found below.

Get your copy of these great books for your Kindle Fire HD or other e-reading devices and pursue your dreams of learning a Spanish today

- Spanish, Learn the Basics by Franco Sanz

- Quick Learn Teach Me Spanish by Clarisa Rodriguez

Made in the USA
San Bernardino, CA
08 December 2013